A BOOK OF
CHRISTMAS VERSE

A BOOK OF
CHRISTMAS VERSE

SELECTED BY H.C. BEECHING
WITH TEN DESIGNS BY WALTER CRANE

BONANZA BOOKS

NEW YORK

Copyright © 1986 by OBC, Inc.

This 1986 edition is published by Bonanza Books,
distributed by Crown Publishers, Inc.,
225 Park Avenue South, New
York, New York 10003.

Printed and Bound in the United States of America

LIBRARY OF CONGRESS CATALOGING-IN-PUBLICATION DATA

A Book of Christmas verse.

Reprint. Originally published: New York : Dodd,
Mead, 1896.
1. Christmas—Poetry. I. Beeching, H. C. (Henry
Charles), 1859–1919.   II. Crane, Walter, 1845–1915.
PN6110.C5B64   1986   821'.008'033   86-17029
ISBN 0-517-61840-0

h g f e d c b a

CONTENTS

CONTENTS

vi

CONTENTS

CONTENTS

CONTENTS

CHRISTMAS MERRYMAKING

CONTENTS

FOREWORD

SINCE THE dawn of man all people of the earth have observed a period when "the days begin to lengthen and the cold begins to strengthen." Now known as the winter solstice, this is the time when the sun, parent of fertility, rises with renewed vigor and power after having been at the lowest point in the heavens.

In ancient England the Druids celebrated this season in their great roofless temples of stone with elaborate ceremonies centering about the mistletoe plant. In the ancient Scandinavian countries great fires were set to defy and ward off the Frost King. Those gathered around the fires would quaff mead and tell strange stories of Valkyrian maidens who searched for souls to bring to Valhalla. The ancient Romans created one great celebration in honor of Saturnus, the god who taught the arts of agriculture and was dedicated to welcoming the germinating impulse of nature.

From these ancient sources plus many others came Christmas, complete with its attendant pageantry, religion, ritual and poetry. In 1896, H. C. Beeching, an esteemed editor, author and poet, prepared an anthology consisting of "whatever poetry in the most modern taste has Christmas for its theme." Clearly, however, the most modern taste of the day covered an incredibly wide range—from Prudentius to Walt Whitman and from John Donne to Sir Walter Scott.

In this astonishing collection one can find Latin hymns, including one by the virtual founder of Latin hymnology; early carols which were compiled during the reign of Henry VI and constitute one of the oldest known collections of Christmas songs; later poems and carols, covering an extensive period from the fourteenth to the nineteenth centuries and reflecting the widely differing tastes and styles of each period; and Christmas merrymaking poems. Mr. Beeching also provided this collection with ten designs by Walter C. Crane, a well-known nineteenth century painter, designer, book illustrator, writer and Socialist; and with a complete section citing the origin of many of the selections presented here.

New York   D.J. DeChristopher
1986

PREFACE

A SUFFICIENT excuse for the preparation of anthologies should be the demand for them. If not, the anthologist may plead further the pleasure they give in the making. In the case of Christmas poems the more proper delight of culling and arranging a nosegay is combined with the zeal of the botanist who hunts shy specimens. The labour of such search is, of course, greatly lightened by the work of previous explorers; and here it is right to acknowledge obligation to two gentlemen, one known only by his initials H. V., the author of a book called 'Christmas with the Poets' (Bell and Daldy, 1862), the other that well-known man of letters, and my good friend, Mr. A. H. Bullen, whose 'Carols and Poems' appeared in a limited edition in 1886 (Nimmo). The differences of the present collection may best be indicated by a comparison with its predecessors. In the first place, it does not, like Mr. Bullen's, appeal to any antiquarian interest. Poems and carols are accepted or rejected simply upon their poetical merit, and for no other reason whatever. Hence such very popular carols as 'The first Nowell,' 'I saw three ships come sailing in,' 'God rest you, merry gentlemen,' and many others, find no admittance; hence too there are

PREFACE

no pieces from Poor Robin's Almanacks; and especially my taste differs from Mr. Bullen's in rejecting altogether the poetry of 'Entire'. Such verses as—

'Bring us in good ale, and bring us in good ale,
For our blessed Lady's sake, bring us in good ale,'

or—

'Here stands my bottle and hook,
   Good kitchen maid, draw near,
Thou art an honest cook,
   And canst draw ale and beer,'

give me no delight; not that I am such a curmudgeon as to grudge Poor Robin his tankard, although the Slys, who 'came in with Richard Conqueror' and are with us still, are seldom very happy or useful members of society, but that I fail to see that any one, except perhaps Herrick, has been 'bemused with beer' to much poetical purpose. In the section of Religious Poems there is more matter common to both; and though my choice has been made independently of Mr. Bullen's book, in the course of reading for a more general 'Lyra Sacra,' it is only fair to say that I have found it ill gleaning behind him in the seventeenth century. About a dozen pieces, however, will be found of that period which are not in his collection. More modern verses, with one or two exceptions, he ignores. H. V.'s book, while it contains a good deal that will be found both in Mr. Bullen's and in

xiv

PREFACE

mine, is remarkable for its selection from the poets of the day; but that day is thirty years past, and its vogue is not ours. Who now reads Alfred Domett, though Browning celebrates him in 'Waring'; or John Clare, whose name has at length been banished from the 'Golden Treasury'; or who can suck rapture out of the broken anapæstic jolt which Eliza Cook's name appeared once to justify?

'The holly, the holly, O twine it with bay,
    Come give the holly a song;
For it helps to drive stern winter away,
    With his garment so sombre and long.

I take the liberty of saying so much because I myself give hostages to my own successor by printing whatever poetry in the most modern taste has Christmas for its theme. I could wish that such pieces were more numerous. To the writers in each case for their courteous permission, as well as to the publishers, I desire to return my humble thanks.

H. C. B.

Yattendon Rectory.

LATIN HYMNS

VENI, Redemptor gentium,
Ostende partum Virginis;
Miretur omne sæculum:
Talis decet partus Deum.

Non ex virili semine,
Sed mystico Spiramine,
Verbum Dei factum est caro,
Fructusque ventris floruit.

Alvus tumescit Virginis,
Claustrum pudoris permanet,
Vexilla virtutum micant,
Versatur in templo Deus.

Procedit e thalamo suo,
Pudoris aulâ regiâ,
Geminae gigas substantiæ,
Alacris ut currat viam.

Egressus ejus a Patre,
Regressus ejus ad Patrem.
Excursus usque ad inferos
Recursus ad sedem Dei.

Aequalis æterno Patri
Carnis stropheo accingere,
Infirma nostri corporis
Virtute firmans perpeti.

LATIN HYMNS

Præsepe jam fulget tuum,
Lumenque nox spirat novum,
Quod nulla nox interpolet,
Fideque jugi luceat.

S. Ambrose.

PUER natus in Bethlehem,
Unde gaudet Jerusalem.

Hic jacet in præsepio,
Qui regnat sine termino.

Cognovit bos et asinus
Quod puer erat Dominus.

Reges de Sabâ veniunt,
Aurum, thus, myrrham offerunt.

Intrantes domum invicem
Novum salutant principem.

De matre natus virgine
Sine virili semine ;

Sine serpentis vulnere
De nostro venit sanguine ;

In carne nobis similis
Peccato sed dissimilis ;

Ut redderet nos homines
Deo et sibi similes.

4

LATIN HYMNS

In hoc natali gaudio
Benedicamus Domino:

Laudetur sancta Trinitas,
Deo dicamus gratias.

HEU quid jaces stabulo
Omnium Creator,
Vagiens cunabulo,
Mundi reparator?
Si rex, ubi purpura,
Vel clientum murmura,
Ubi aula regis?
Hic omnis penuria,
Paupertatis curia,
Forma novæ legis.

Istuc amor generis
Me traxit humani,
Quod se noxâ sceleris
Occidit profani.
His meis inopiis
Gratiarum copiis
Te pergo ditare;
Hocce natalitio,
Vero sacrificio
Te volens beare.

O te laudum millibus
Laudo, laudo, laudo;

LATIN HYMNS

Tantis mirabilibus
Plaudo, plaudo, plaudo :
Gloria, sit gloria,
Amanti memoria
Domino in altis :
Cui testimonia
Dantur et præconia
Cœlicis a psaltis.

                                   John Mauburn.

ADESTE fideles,
    Læti triumphantes,
Venite, venite in Bethlehem ;
    Natum videte,
    Regem angelorum,
Venite, adoremus Dominum.

    Deum de Deo,
    Lumen de Lumine,
Gestant puellæ viscera,
    Deum verum,
    Genitum non factum ;
Venite, adoremus Dominum.

    En, grege relicto
    Humiles ad cunas
Vocati pastores approperant ;
    Et nos ovanti
    Gradu festinemus,
Venite, adoremus Dominum.

6

LATIN HYMNS

Stella duce, Magi
Christum adorantes,
Aurum, thus, et myrrham dant munera ;
Jesu infanti
Corda præbeamus :
Venite, adoremus Dominum.

Æterni Parentis
Splendorem æternum
Velatum sub carne videbimus,
Deum infantem
Pannis involutum ;
Venite, adoremus Dominum.

Pro nobis egenum
Et fæno cubantem
Piis foveamus amplexibus ;
Sic nos amantem
Quis non redameret ?
Venite, adoremus Dominum.

Cantet nunc hymnos
Chorus angelorum,
Cantet nunc aula cælestium :—
Gloria
In excelsis Deo :
Venite, adoremus Dominum.

Ergo qui natus
Die hodierna,

LATIN HYMNS

Jesu, tibi sit gloria
    Patris æterni
    Verbum caro factum !
Venite, adoremus Dominum.

CORDE natus ex Parentis
Ante mundi exordium,
Alpha et oo cognominatus,
Ipse fons et clausula.
Omnium quæ sunt, fuerunt,
Quæque post futura sunt
    Sæculorum sæculis.

Ecce quem vates vetustis
Concinebant sæculis,
Quem prophetarum fideles
Paginæ spoponderant,
Emicat promissus olim,
Cunctaque collaudent Deum
    Sæculorum sæculis.

O beatus ortus ille,
Virgo cum puerpera
Edidit nostram salutem
Feta sancto Spiritu,
Et puer Redemptor orbis
Os sacratum protulit
    Sæculorum sæculis.

8

LATIN HYMNS

Psallat altitudo cæli,
Psallant omnes angeli,
Quicquid est virtutis usquam
Psallat in laudem Dei ;
Nulla linguarum silescat,
Vox et omnis personet
    Sæculorum sæculis.

Te senes, et te juventus,
Parvulorum te cohors,
Turba matrum, virginumque
Simplices puellulæ,
Voce concordes pudicis
Perstrepant concentibus
    Sæculorum sæculis.

Tibi, Christe, sit cum Patre
Agioque Spiritu,
Hymnus, melos, laus perennis,
Gratiarum actio,
Honor, virtus, et victoria,
Regnum, æternaliter
    Sæculorum sæculis.

Prudentius.

NOWELL, nowell, nowell, nowell,
Missus est ad virginem angelus Gabriel.

Angelum misit suum Deus omnipotens,
Ut unicum per filium ejus salvetur gens.

LATIN HYMNS

Virgo ave, clamat ille, O Maria clemens,
Concipies et paries, virgo semper manens.

Virgo clam tremescit, nam mira valde audit,
Eam cui est ille missus comfortavit.
Altissimi Patris tui virtus obumbravit.
Cui per flamen sacrum gramen in te seminavit.

Virgo clemens semper tremens ad verba angeli,
Cui flamen consolamen dat responsum illi,
Miti voce dicens, Ecce ancilla Domini,
Et secundum tuum verbum, ita fiat mihi.

Virgo Deum genuit verbum, quem alit cum cura,
Mirus Pater, mira Mater, mira Genitura;
Parit virgo solo verbo contra carnis jura,
Perseverante post et ante virgine pura.

Nobis natus, nobis datus, quem virgo lactavit,
Atque gregi, sic sub lege cunctaque creavit,
Miti corde nos a sorde moriendo lavavit;
Miserere plebi tuæ, Jhesu fili Davit.

Virgo pia, O Maria, pura ut lilia
Sponsa Dei, soror ei, mater et filia,
Tu Hunc ores, viatores ut fugiant vilia,
Et nos trahant huc quo gaudent sanctorum milia.

EARLY CAROLS

I SING of a maiden
   That is makeless;[1]
King of all kings
   To her son she ches;[2]
He came also[3] still
   There his mother was,
As dew in April
   That falleth on the grass.
He came also still
   To his mother's bower,
As dew in April
   That falleth on the flower.
He came also still
   There his mother lay,
As dew in April
   That falleth on the spray.
Mother and maiden
   Was never none but she;
Well may such a lady
   God's mother be.

AS Joseph was a-walking
   He heard an angel sing:—
'This night shall be born
   Our heavenly King;

---

[1] Matchless.   [2] Chose.   [3] As.

EARLY CAROLS

' He neither shall be born
   In housen nor in hall,
Nor in the place of Paradise,
   But in an ox's stall;

' He neither shall be clothed
   In purple nor in pall,
But all in fair linen
   As were babies all.

' He neither shall be rocked
   In silver nor in gold,
But in a wooden cradle
   That rocks on the mould.

' He neither shall be christened
   In white wine or red,
But with fair spring water
   With which we were christenèd.'

NAY, ivy, nay,
   It shall not be, i-wis;[1]
Let holly have the mastery,
   As the manner is.

Holly stand in the hall,
   Fair to behold;
Ivy stand without the door,
   She is full sore a-cold,
          Nay, ivy, nay, etc.

---

[1] Certainly.

14

EARLY CAROLS

Holly and his merry men,
　They dancen and they sing;
Ivy and her maidens
　They weepen and they wring.
　　　　　Nay, ivy, nay, etc.

Ivy hath a kybe,[1]
　She caught it with the cold;
So mot they all have ae,[2]
　That with ivy hold.
　　　　　Nay, ivy, nay, etc.

Holly hath berries
　As red as any rose,
The foster[3] [and] the hunters
　Keep them from the does.
　　　　　Nay, ivy, nay, etc.

Ivy hath berries
　As black as any sloe;
There come the owl
　And eat him as she go.
　　　　　Nay, ivy, nay, etc.

Holly hath birdès,
　A full fair flock,
The nightingale, the popinjay,
　The gentle laverock.
　　　　　Nay, ivy, nay, etc.

---

[1] Chilblain.　　　[2] Every one.　　　[3] Forester.

EARLY CAROLS

Good ivy,
  What birdès hast thou?
None but the howlet
  That krey [1] 'how, how.'

Nay, ivy, nay,
  It shall not be, i-wis;
Let holly have the mastery
  As the manner is.

IN Bethlehem that noble place,
As by prophecy said it was,
Of the Virgin Mary full of grace,
Salvator mundi natus est.
      Be we merry in this feast,
      In quo Salvator natus est.

On Christmas night an angel it told
To the shepherds, keeping their fold,
That into Bethlehem with beasts wold, [2]
Salvator mundi natus est.
      Be we merry, etc.

The shepherdès were compassed right,
About them was a full great light;
Dread ye nought, said the angel bright,
Salvator mundi natus est.
      Be we merry, etc.

---

[1] Cries.   [2] Wild.

16

EARLY CAROLS

Behold to you we bring great joy;
For why [1] Jesus is born this day;
To us, of Mary, that mild May,
Salvator mundi natus est.
>> Be we merry, etc.

And thus in faith find it ye shall,
Lying poorly in an oxës-stall.
The shepherds then God lauded all,
Quia Salvator mundi natus est.
>> Be we merry, etc.

>> THIS endris [2] night
>> I saw a sight,
>> A star as bright as day;
>> And ever among
>> A maiden sung,
>>> Lullay, byby, lullay.

This lovely lady sat and sang, and to her childë said—
'My son, my brother, my father dear, why liest
> thou thus in hayd? [3]
>> My sweetë brid, [4]
>> Thus it is betid
>>> Though thou be King veray;
>> But, nevertheless,
>> I will not cease
>>> To sing byby, lullay.'

---

[1] Because.   [2] Last.   [3] Hay.   [4] Bird.

EARLY CAROLS

The child then spake; in his talking he to his
    mother said—
'I bekid[1] am king, in crib though I be laid;
        For angels bright
        Down to me light,
          Thou knowest it is no nay.
        And of that sight
        Thou mayest be light,
          To sing byby, lullay.'

'Now, sweet son, since thou art king, why art thou
    laid in stall?
Why not thou ordain thy bedding in some great
    king's hall?
        Methinketh it is right
        That king or knight
          Should be in good array;
        And them among
        It were no wrong
          To sing byby, lullay.'

'Mary, mother, I am thy child, though I be laid in
    stall,
Lords and dukes shall worship me, and so shall
    kingës all.
        Ye shall well see,
        That kingës three,
          Shall come on the twelfth day;
        For this behest
        Give me thy breast,
          And sing byby, lullay.'

---

[1] Signified, p.p. of 'bekinnen.'

EARLY CAROLS

'Now tell me, sweet son, I thee pray, thou art my
    love and dear,
How should I keep thee to thy pay,[1] and make thee
    glad of cheer?
        For all thy will
        I would fulfil,
            Thou weet'st full well in fay.[2]
        And for all this
        I will thee kiss,
            And sing byby, lullay.'

'My dear mother, when time it be, take thou me
    up aloft,
And set me upon thy knee, and handle me full soft.
        And in thy arm
        Thou wilt me warm,
            And keep night and day;
        If I weep
        And may not sleep,
            Thou sing byby, lullay.'

'Now, sweet son, since it is so, all things are at
    thy will,
I pray thee grant to me a boon if it be right and skill,
        That child or man,
        That will and can,
            Be merry upon my day;
        To bliss them bring,
        And I shall sing
            Lullay, byby, lullay.

---

[1] Content.   [2] Faith.

S. Stephen

EARLY CAROLS

SAINT STEPHEN was a clerk
  In King Herodës hall,
And servèd him of bread and cloth
  As ever king befall.

Stephen out of kitchen came,
  With boarës head on hand,
He saw a star was fair and bright
  Over Bethlehem stand.

He kist[1] adown the boarës head
  And went into the hall:
'I forsake thee, King Herod,
  And thy workès all.

'I forsake thee, King Herod,
  And thy workès all;
There is a child in Bethlehem born
  Is better than we all.'

'What aileth thee, Stephen?
  What is thee befall?
Lacketh thee either meat or drink
  In King Herodës hall?'

'Lacketh me neither meat ne drink
  In King Herodës hall;
There is a child in Bethlehem born
  Is better than we all.'

---

[1] Cast.

EARLY CAROLS

'What aileth thee, Stephen?
    Art thou wode[1] or thou ginnest to breed?[2]
Lacketh thee either gold or fee
    Or any richë weed?'[3]

'Lacketh me neither gold or fee,
    Ne none richë weed;
There is a child in Bethlehem born
    Shall helpen us at our need.'

'That is al so[4] sooth, Stephen,
    Al so sooth, i-wis,[5]
As this capon crowè shall
    That lieth here in my dish.'

That word was not so soon said,
    That word in that hall,
The capon crew, 'Christus natus est,'
    Among the lordès all.

'Riseth up, my tormentors,
    By two and all by one,
And leadeth Stephen out of this town,
    And stoneth him with stone.'

Tooken they then Stephen
    And stoned him in the way,
And therefore is his even
    On Christès own day.

---

[1] Mad. [2] Upbraid. [3] Dress. [4] As. [5] Certainly.

LATER POEMS AND CAROLS

OF THE NATIVITY OF CHRIST

Rorate Cœli desuper!
  Heavens distil your balmy showers,
For now is risen the bright daystar
  From the Rose Mary, flower of flowers;
  The clear sun, whom no cloud devours,
Surmounting Phœbus in the east,
  Is comen of his heavenly towers;
Et nobis Puer natus est.

Archangels, angels, dominations,
  Thrones, potentates, and martyrs seir,[1]
And all the heavenly operations,
  Star, planet, firmament, and sphere,
  Fire, earth, air, and water clear,
To Him give loving, most and least,
  That come is in so meek maneir;
Et nobis Puer natus est.

Sinners be glad, and penance do,
  And thank your Maker heartily,
For He, that ye might not come to,
  To you is comen full humbly,
  Your soulës with His blood to buy,

---

[1] Many.

OF THE NATIVITY OF CHRIST

And loose you of the fiend's arrest,
  And only of His own mercy;
Pro nobis Puer natus est.

Celestial fowlës in the air,
  Sing with your notes upon hight,
In firthës and forests fair.
  Be mirthful now, at all your might,
  For passed is your dully night;
Aurora has the cloudis perced,
  The sun is risen with gladsome light,
Et nobis Puer natus est.

Now spring up flowrës from the root,
  Revert you upward naturally,
In honour of the blessed fruit
  That rose up from the Rose Mary;
  Lay out your leavës lustily,
From dead take life now, at the least,
  In worship of that Prince worthy,
Qui nobis Puer natus est.

Sing heaven imperial, most of height,
  Regions of air make harmony;
All fish in floud, and fowl of flight,
  Be mirthful and make melody;
  All Gloria in Excelsis cry,
Heaven, earth, sea, man, bird, and beast,
  He that is crowned above the sky.
Pro nobis Puer natus est.

W. Dunbar.

The·Burning·Babe·

As I in hoary winter's night stood shivering in the
    snow,
Surprised I was with sudden heat which made my
    heart to glow ;
And lifting up a fearful eye to view what fire was
    near,
A pretty Babe all burning bright did in the air
    appear.
Who scorchèd with exceeding heat such floods of
    tears did shed,
As though His floods should quench his flames
    with what His tears were fed ;

27

THE BURNING BABE

Alas, quoth He, but newly born in fiery heats of fry,
Yet none approach to warm their hearts or feel my
    fire but I.
My faultless breast the furnace is, the fuel wound-
    ing thorns,
Love is the fire, and sighs the smoke, the ashes
    shame and scorns ;
The fuel Justice layeth on, and Mercy blows the
    coals ;
The metal in this furnace wrought are men's
    defilèd souls ;
For which, as now on fire I am, to work them to
    their good,
So will I melt into a bath, to wash them in my
    blood :
With this He vanished out of sight, and swiftly
    shrunk away,
And straight I callèd unto mind that it was
    Christmas day.

                        Robert Southwell.

NEW PRINCE, NEW POMP

Behold a silly tender Babe,
  In freezing winter night,
In homely manger trembling lies
  Alas ! a piteous sight.

28

NEW PRINCE, NEW POMP

The inns are full, no man will yield
   This little Pilgrim bed ;
But forced He is with silly beasts
   In crib to shroud His head.

Despise Him not for lying there,
   First what He is inquire ;
An orient pearl is often found
   In depth of dirty mire.

Weigh not His crib, His wooden dish,
   Nor beast that by Him feed ;
Weigh not His mother's poor attire,
   Nor Joseph's simple weed.

This stable is a prince's court,
   This crib His chair of state ;
The beasts are parcel of His pomp,
   The wooden dish His plate.

The persons in that poor attire
   His royal liveries wear ;
The Prince Himself is come from heaven,
   This pomp is prizèd there.

With joy approach, O Christian wight !
   Do homage to thy King ;
And highly praise this humble pomp
   Which He from heaven doth bring.

NEW HEAVEN, NEW WAR

Come to your heaven, you heavenly quires !
Earth hath the heaven of your desires :
Remove your dwelling to your God,
A stall is now His best abode ;
Sith men their homage do deny,
Come, angels, all their faults supply.

His chilling cold doth heat require,
Come, Seraphim, in lieu of fire ;
This little ark no cover hath,
Let Cherubs' wings His body swathe ;
Come, Raphael, this Babe must eat,
Provide our little Tobie meat.

Let Gabriel be now His groom,
That first took up His earthly room ;
Let Michael stand in His defence,
Whom love hath linked to feeble sense ;
Let Graces rock when He doth cry,
And Angels sing His lullaby.

The same you saw in heavenly seat,
Is He that now sucks Mary's teat ;
Agnize[1] your King a mortal wight,
His borrowed weeds lets[2] not your sight ;

---

[1] Acknowledge.   [2] Hinders.

NEW HEAVEN, NEW WAR

Come, kiss the manger where He lies;
That is your bliss above the skies.

This little Babe so few days old,
Is come to rifle Satan's fold,
All hell doth at His presence quake,
Though He Himself for cold do shake;
For in this weak unarmèd wise
The gates of hell He will surprise.

With tears He fights and wins the field,
His naked breast stands for a shield;
His battering shot are babish cries;
His arrows, looks of weeping eyes;
His martial ensigns, cold and need;
And feeble flesh His warrior's steed.

His camp is pitchèd in a stall,
His bulwark but a broken wall,
His crib His trench, hay-stalks His stakes,
Of shepherds He His muster takes;
And thus, as sure His foe to wound,
The angels' trumps alarum sound.

My soul, with Christ join thou in fight;
Stick to the tents that He hath pight;
Within His crib is surest ward,
This little Babe will be thy guard;
If thou wilt foil thy foes with joy,
Then flit not from this heavenly Boy.

A CHILD MY CHOICE

A CHILD MY CHOICE

Let folly praise that fancy loves,
  I praise and love that Child,
Whose heart no thought, whose tongue no word,
  Whose head no deed defiled.

I praise Him most, I love Him best,
  All praise and love is His;
While Him I love, in Him I live,
  And cannot live amiss.

Love's sweetest mark, laud's highest theme,
  Man's most desirèd light,
To love Him life, to leave Him death,
  To live in Him delight.

He mine by gift, I His by debt,
  Thus each to other due,
First friend He was, best friend He is,
  All times will try Him true.

Though young, yet wise; though small, yet strong;
  Though man, yet God He is;
As wise He knows, as strong He can,
  As God He loves to bless.

32

NATIVITY

His knowledge rules, His strength defends,
   His love doth cherish all;
His birth our joy, His life our light,
   His death our end of thrall.

Alas! He weeps, He sighs, He pants,
   Yet doth His angels sing;
Out of His tears, His sighs and throbs,
   Doth bud a joyful spring.

Almighty Babe, whose tender arms
   Can force all foes to fly,
Correct my faults, protect my life,
   Direct me when I die!

NATIVITY

Immensity, cloister'd in thy dear womb,
Now leaves his well-beloved imprisonment;
There He hath made Himself to his intent,
Weak enough now into our world to come:
But oh! for thee, for Him, hath th' inn no room?
Yet lay Him in His stall, and from th' orient
Stars and wise men will travel, to prevent
Th' effect of Herod's jealous general doom.
See'st thou, my soul! with thy faith's eye, how He,
Which fills all place, yet none holds Him, doth lie!

33

FOR CHRISTMAS DAY

Was not His pity towards thee wondrous high,
That would have need to be pitied by thee?
Kiss Him, and with Him into Egypt go,
With His kind mother who partakes thy woe.

John Donne.

FOR CHRISTMAS DAY

Immortal Babe, who this dear day
Didst change Thine heaven for our clay,
And didst with flesh Thy godhead veil,
Eternal Son of God, all hail!

Shine, happy star; ye angels, sing
Glory on high to heaven's King:
Run, shepherds, leave your nightly watch,
See heaven come down to Bethlehem's cratch.

Worship, ye sages of the east,
The King of gods in meanness dressed,
O blessèd maid, smile and adore
The God thy womb and arms have bore.

Star, angels, shepherds, and wise sages,
Thou virgin glory of all ages,
Restorèd frame of heaven and earth,
Joy in your dear Redeemer's birth!

Bishop Hall.

34

AN HYMN ON THE NATIVITY OF MY SAVIOUR

I sing the birth was born to-night,
The Author both of life and light,
    The angel so did sound it:
And like the ravished shepherds said,
Who saw the light and were afraid,
    Yet searched, and true they found it.

The Son of God, th' Eternal King,
That did us all salvation bring,
    And freed the soul from danger;
He whom the whole world could not take,
The Word, which heaven and earth did make,
    Was now laid in a manger.

The Father's wisdom willed it so,
The Son's obedience knew no No,
    Both wills were in one stature;
And as that wisdom had decreed,
The Word was now made flesh indeed,
    And took on Him our nature.

What comfort by Him do we win,
Who made Himself the price of sin
    To make us heirs of glory!
To see this Babe, all innocence,
A martyr born in our defence:
    Can man forget the story?

Ben Jonson.
35

OF THE EPIPHANY

Fair eastern star, that art ordained to run
Before the sages, to the rising sun,
Here cease thy course, and wonder that the cloud
Of this poor stable can thy Maker shroud:
Ye heavenly bodies glory to be bright,
And are esteemed as ye are rich in light,
But here on earth is taught a different way,
Since under this low roof the Highest lay.
Jerusalem erects her stately towers,
Displays her windows and adorns her bowers;
Yet there thou must not cast a trembling spark,
Let Herod's palace still continue dark;
Each school and synagogue thy force repels,
There Pride enthroned in misty error dwells;
The temple, where the priests maintain their quire,
Shall taste no beam of thy celestial fire,
While this weak cottage all thy splendour takes:
A joyful gate of every chink it makes.
Here shines no golden roof, no ivory stair,
No king exalted in a stately chair,
Girt with attendants, or by heralds styled,
But straw and hay enwrap a speechless Child.
Yet Sabae's lords before this Babe unfold
Their treasures, offering incense, myrrh, and gold.

The crib becomes an altar: therefore dies
No ox nor sheep; for in their fodder lies

36

OF THE EPIPHANY

The Prince of Peace, who, thankful for His bed,
Destroys those rites in which their blood was shed:
The quintessence of earth he takes, and fees,
And precious gums distilled from weeping trees;
Rich metals and sweet odours now declare
The glorious blessings which His laws prepare,
To clear us from the base and loathsome flood
Of sense, and make us fit for angels' food,
Who lift to God for us the holy smoke
Of fervent prayers with which we Him invoke,
And try our actions in the searching fire,
By which the seraphims our lips inspire:
No muddy dross pure minerals shall infect,
We shall exhale our vapours up direct:
No storm shall cross, nor glittering lights deface
Perpetual sighs which seek a happy place.

Sir John Beaumont.

The Angels

THE ANGELS

Run, shepherds, run, where Bethlehem blest
   appears.
  We bring the best of news ; be not dismayed ;
A Saviour there is born more old than years,
  Amidst heaven's rolling height this earth who
   stayed.
  In a poor cottage inned, a virgin maid
A weakling did Him bear, Who all upbears ;
  There is He poorly swaddled, in manger laid,
To whom too narrow swaddlings are our spheres :
Run, shepherds, run, and solemnise His birth.
  This is that night—no, day, grown great with
   bliss,
  In which the power of Satan broken is :
In heaven be glory, peace unto the earth !
  Thus singing, through the air the angels swam,
  And cope of stars re-echoèd the same.

William Drummond
of Hawthornden.

THE SHEPHERDS

THE SHEPHERDS

O than the fairest day, thrice fairer night!
  Night to blest days in which a sun doth rise,
  Of which that golden eye which clears the skies
Is but a sparkling ray, a shadow-light!
And blessed ye, in silly pastor's sight,
  Mild creatures, in whose warm crib now lies
That heaven-sent Youngling, holy-maid-born
      Wight,
Midst, end, beginning of our prophecies!
Blest cottage that hath flowers in winter spread,
  Though withered — blessed grass that hath the
      grace
  To deck and be a carpet to that place!
Thus sang, unto the sounds of oaten reed,
  Before the Babe, the shepherds bowed on knees,
  And springs ran nectar, honey dropped from trees.

A Rocking Hymn

Sweet baby, sleep! What ails my dear?
  What ails my darling thus to cry?
Be still, my child, and lend thine ear
  To hear me sing thy lullaby.
      My pretty lamb, forbear to weep;
      Be still, my dear; sweet baby, sleep!

Thou blessèd soul, what canst thou fear?
  What thing to thee can mischief do?
Thy God is now Thy Father dear;
  His holy spouse thy mother too.
      Sweet baby, then, forbear to weep;
      Be still, my babe; sweet baby, sleep!

41

A ROCKING HYMN

Whilst thus thy lullaby I sing,
  For thee great blessings ripening be ;
Thine Eldest Brother is a King,
  And hath a kingdom bought for thee.
      Sweet baby, then, forbear to weep ;
      Be still, my babe ; sweet baby, sleep.

Sweet baby, sleep, and nothing fear ;
  For whosoever thee offends
By thy protector threatened are,
  And God and angels are thy friends,
      Sweet baby, then, forbear to weep ;
      Be still, my babe ; sweet baby, sleep.

When God with us was dwelling here,
  In little babes He took delight :
Such innocents as thou, my dear,
  Are ever precious in His sight.
      Sweet baby, then, forbear to weep ;
      Be still, my babe ; sweet baby, sleep.

A little Infant once was He,
  And strength in weakness then was laid
Upon His virgin-mother's knee,
  That power to thee might be conveyed.
      Sweet baby, then, forbear to weep ;
      Be still, my babe ; sweet baby, sleep.

In this thy frailty and thy need
  He friends and helpers doth prepare,

A ROCKING HYMN

Which thee shall cherish, clothe, and feed,
  For of thy weal they tender are.
    Sweet baby, then, forbear to weep;
    Be still, my babe; sweet baby, sleep.

The King of kings, when He was born,
  Had not so much for outward ease;
By Him such dressings were not worn,
  Nor such like swaddling-clothes as these.
    Sweet baby, then, forbear to weep;
    Be still, my babe; sweet baby, sleep.

Within a manger lodged thy Lord,
  Where oxen lay and asses fed;
Warm rooms we do to thee afford,
  An easy cradle or a bed.
    Sweet baby, then, forbear to weep;
    Be still, my babe; sweet baby, sleep.

The wants that He did then sustain
  Have purchased wealth, my babe, for thee;
And by His torments and His pain
  Thy rest and ease securèd be.
    My baby, then, forbear to weep;
    Be still, my babe; sweet baby, sleep.

Thou hast, yet more, to perfect this,
  A promise and an earnest got
Of gaining everlasting bliss,
  Though thou, my babe, perceiv'st it not.
    Sweet baby, then, forbear to weep;
    Be still, my babe; sweet baby, sleep.

George Wither.

GLORIA IN EXCELSIS

As on the night before this happy morn,
  A blessèd angel unto shepherds told
Where (in a stable) He was poorly born,
Whom nor the earth nor heaven of heavens can hold:
    Thro' Bethlehem rung
      This news at their return;
    Yea, angels sung
      That God with us was born;
And they made mirth because we should not mourn.
    Their angel carol sing we, then,
      To God on high all glory be,
      For peace on earth bestoweth He,
    And sheweth favour unto men.

This favour Christ vouchsafèd for our sake;
  To buy us thrones, He in a manger lay;
Our weakness took, that we His strength might
      take;
  And was disrobed that He might us array;
    Our flesh He wore,
      Our sin to wear away;
    Our curse He bore,
      That we escape it may:
And wept for us, that we might sing for aye.
    With angels therefore, sing again,
      To God on high all glory be,
      For peace on earth bestoweth He,
    And sheweth favour unto men.

44

WHO CAN FORGET

WHO CAN FORGET

Who can forget—never to be forgot—
The time, that all the world in slumber lies,
When, like the stars, the singing angels shot
To earth, and heaven awakèd all his eyes
To see another sun at midnight rise
  On earth? Was never sight of pareil fame,
  For God before man like Himself did frame,
But God Himself now like a mortal man became.

A Child He was, and had not learnt to speak,
That with His word the world before did make ;
His mother's arms Him bore, He was so weak,
That with one hand the vaults of heaven could
      shake,
See how small room my infant Lord doth take,
  Whom all the world is not enough to hold !
  Who of His years, or of His age hath told ?
Never such age so young, never a child so old.

And yet but newly He was infanted,
And yet already He was sought to die ;
Yet scarcely born, already banishèd ;
Not able yet to go, and forced to fly :
But scarcely fled away, when by and by
  The tyrant's sword with blood is all defiled,
  And Rachel, for her sons, with fury wild,
Cries, 'O thou cruel king, and O my sweetest child !'

Egypt His nurse became, where Nilus springs,
Who, straight to entertain the rising sun,

45

A CHRISTMAS CAROL

The hasty harvest in his bosom brings ;
But now for drought the fields were all undone,
And now with waters all is overrun :
   So fast the Cynthian mountains pour'd their snow,
   When once they felt the sun so near them glow,
That Nilus Egypt lost, and to a sea did grow.

The angels carolled loud their song of peace ;
The cursèd oracles were strucken dumb ;
To see their Shepherd the poor shepherds press ;
To see their King the kingly sophies come ;
And them to guide unto his Master's home,
   A star comes dancing up the orient,
   That springs for joy over the strawy tent,
Where gold, to make their Prince a crown, they all
     present.

Giles Fletcher.

A CHRISTMAS CAROL

[Sung to the King in the Presence at Whitehall.]
Chor.—What sweeter music can we bring
Than a carol, for to sing
The birth of this our heavenly King?
Awake the voice! awake the string!
Heart, ear, and eye, and every thing
Awake! the while the active finger
Runs divisions with the singer.

[From the flourish they come to the song.]

Dark and dull night, fly hence away,
And give the honour to this day,
That sees December turn'd to May.

46

ON THE BIRTH OF OUR SAVIOUR

If we may ask the reason, say
The why and wherefore all things here
Seem like the spring-time of the year?
Why does the chilling winter's morn
Smile like a field beset with corn?
Or smell like to a mead new shorn,

Thus on a sudden? Come and see
The cause why things thus fragrant be:
'Tis He is born whose quickening birth
Gives life and lustre public mirth,
To heaven and the under-earth.

Chor.—We see Him come, and know Him ours,
Who with His sunshine and His showers
Turns all the patient ground to flowers.

The Darling of the world is come,
And fit it is we find a room
To welcome Him.   The nobler part
Of all the house here is the heart.

Chor.—Which we will give Him; and bequeath
This holly and this ivy wreath,
To do him honour; who's our King,
And Lord of all this revelling.

Robert Herrick.

AN ODE ON THE BIRTH OF OUR SAVIOUR

In numbers, and but these few,
I sing Thy birth, O Jesu!
Thou pretty Baby, born here
With sup'rabundant scorn here:

ON THE BIRTH OF OUR SAVIOUR

Who for Thy princely port here,
    Hadst for Thy place
    Of birth, a base
Out-stable for Thy court here.

Instead of neat enclosures
Of interwoven osiers,
Instead of fragrant posies
Of daffodils and roses,
Thy cradle, kingly Stranger,
    As gospel tells,
    Was nothing else
But here a homely manger.

But we with silks not crewels,
With sundry precious jewels,
And lily work will dress Thee;
And, as we dispossess Thee
Of clouts, we 'll make a chamber,
    Sweet Babe, for Thee,
    Of ivory,
And plaster'd round with amber.

The Jews they did disdain Thee,
But we will entertain Thee,
With glories to await here
Upon Thy princely state here,
And, more for love than pity,
    From year to year
    We 'll make Thee here
A free-born of our city.

CHRISTMAS

CHRISTMAS

All after pleasures as I rid one day,
  My horse and I both tired, body and mind,
  With full cry of affections quite astray,
I took up in the next inn I could find.

There, when I came, whom found I but my dear—
  My dearest Lord ; expecting till the grief
  Of pleasures brought me to Him ; ready there
To be all passengers' most sweet relief?

O Thou, whose glorious, yet contracted, light,
  Wrapt in night's mantle, stole into a manger ;
  Since my dark soul and brutish is Thy right,
To man, of all beasts, be not Thou a stranger.

Furnish and deck my soul, that Thou may'st have
A better lodging than a rack or grave.

The shepherds sing ; and shall I silent be ?
  My God, no hymn for thee ?
My soul's a shepherd too ; a flock it feeds
  Of thoughts and words and deeds.
The pasture is Thy word, the streams Thy grace,
  Enriching every place.

Shepherd and flock shall sing, and all my powers
  Outsing the daylight hours.

On the Morning of Christ's Nativity

THE MORNING OF CHRIST'S NATIVITY

Then we will chide the sun for letting night
  Take up his place and right:
We sing one common Lord; wherefore he should
  Himself the candle hold.

I will go searching till I find a sun
  Shall stay till we have done;
A willing shiner, that shall shine as gladly
  As frost-nipt suns look sadly.
Then we will sing and shine all our own day,
  And one another pay.

His beams shall cheer my breast, and both so twine,
Till ev'n His beams sing and my music shine.

George Herbert.

ON THE MORNING OF CHRIST'S NATIVITY

This is the month, and this the happy morn,
Wherein the Son of heaven's eternal King,
Of wedded Maid and Virgin-Mother born,
Our great redemption from above did bring;
For so the holy sages once did sing,
    That He our deadly forfeit should release,
And with His Father work us a perpetual peace.

That glorious form, that light unsufferable,
And that far-beaming blaze of majesty,

51

ON THE MORNING

Wherewith he wont at heaven's high council-table
To sit the midst of Trinal Unity,
He laid aside; and, here with us to be,
    Forsook the courts of everlasting day,
And chose with us a darksome house of mortal clay.

Say, heavenly Muse, shall not thy sacred vein
Afford a present to the Infant God?
Hast thou no verse, no hymn, or solemn strain,
To welcome Him to this His new abode,
Now while the heaven, by the sun's team untrod,
    Hath took no print of the approaching light,
And all the spangled host kept watch in squadrons
      bright?

See, how from far, upon the eastern road,
The star-led wizards haste with odours sweet;
O run, prevent them with thy humble ode,
And lay it lowly at His blessed feet;
Have thou the honour first thy Lord to greet,
    And join thy voice unto the angel-quire,
From out His secret altar touch'd with hallow'd fire.

THE HYMN

It was the winter wild,
While the heaven-born Child
    All meanly wrapt in the rude manger lies;
Nature in awe to Him,
Had doff'd her gaudy trim,
    With her great Master so to sympathise:

52

OF CHRIST'S NATIVITY

It was no season then for her
To wanton with the sun, her lusty paramour.

Only with speeches fair,
She woos the gentle air
    To hide her guilty front with innocent snow,
And on her naked shame,
Pollute with sinful blame,
    The saintly veil of maiden-white to throw;
Confounded, that her Maker's eyes
Should look so near upon her foul deformities.

But He, her fears to cease,
Sent down the meek-eyed Peace;
    She, crown'd with olive green, came softly
      sliding
Down through the turning sphere,
His ready harbinger,
    With turtle wing the amorous clouds dividing;
And waving wide her myrtle wand,
She strikes an universal peace through sea and
      land.

No war, or battle's sound,
Was heard the world around:
    The idle spear and shield were high up-hung,
The hooked chariot stood
Unstain'd with hostile blood;
    The trumpet spake not to the armed throng,
And kings sat still with awful eye,
As if they surely knew their sovran Lord was by.

ON THE MORNING

But peaceful was the night
Wherein the Prince of Light
    His reign of peace upon the earth began :
The winds with wonder whist
Smoothly the waters kist,
    Whispering new joys to the mild ocean,
Who now hath quite forgot to rave,
While birds of calm sit brooding on the charmed
      wave.

The stars with deep amaze
Stand fix'd in steadfast gaze,
    Bending one way their precious influence,
And will not take their flight
For all the morning light,
    Or Lucifer that often warn'd them thence ;
But in their glimmering orbs did glow,
Until their Lord Himself bespake, and bid them go.

And though the shady gloom
Had given day her room,
    The sun himself withheld his wonted speed,
And hid his head for shame,
As his inferior flame
    The new enlighten'd world no more should
      need ;
He saw a greater Sun appear
Than his bright throne, or burning axletree could
      bear.

OF CHRIST'S NATIVITY

The shepherds on the lawn
Or ere the point of dawn
    Sat simply chatting in a rustic row;
Full little thought they then
That the mighty Pan
    Was kindly come to live with them below;
Perhaps their loves, or else their sheep,
Was all that did their silly thoughts so busy keep.

When such music sweet
Their hearts and ears did greet,
    As never was by mortal finger strook;
Divinely-warbled voice
Answering the stringed noise,
    As all their souls in blissful rapture took:
The air such pleasure loth to lose,
With thousand echoes still prolongs each heavenly
      close.

Nature that heard such sound,
Beneath the hollow round
    Of Cynthia's seat, the airy region thrilling,
Now was almost won
To think her part was done,
    And that her reign had here its last fulfilling;
She knew such harmony alone
Could hold all heaven and earth in happier union.

At last surrounds their sight
A globe of circular light,
    That with long beams the shamefaced night
      array'd;

ON THE MORNING

The helmed Cherubim,
The sworded Seraphim,
    Are seen in glittering ranks with wings dis-
        play'd,
Harping in loud and solemn quire,
With unexpressive notes to Heaven's new-born
        Heir.

Such music as ('tis said)
Before was never made,
    But when of old the sons of morning sung,
While the Creator great
His constellations set,
    And the well-balanced world on hinges hung,
And cast the dark foundations deep,
And bid the weltering waves their oozy channel
        keep.

Ring out, ye crystal spheres,
Once bless our human ears,
    (If ye have power to touch our senses so ;)
And let your silver chime
Move in melodious time,
    And let the base of heaven's deep organ blow ;
And with your ninefold harmony
Make up full consort to the angelic symphony.

For if such holy song
Enwrap our fancy long,
    Time will run back, and fetch the age of gold ;
And speckled Vanity

56

OF CHRIST'S NATIVITY

Will sicken soon and die,
 And leprous Sin will melt from earthly mould ;
And Hell itself will pass away,
And leave her dolorous mansions to the peering day.

Yea, Truth and Justice then
Will down return to men.
 Orb'd in a rainbow ; and, like glories wearing,
Mercy will sit between,
Throned in celestial sheen,
  With radiant feet the tissued clouds down
   steering ;
And heaven, as at some festival,
Will open wide the gates of her high palace-hall.

But wisest Fate says no,
This must not yet be so,
 The Babe yet lies in smiling infancy,
That on the bitter cross
Must redeem our loss ;
 So both Himself and us to glorify :
Yet first to those ychain'd in sleep,
The wakeful trump of doom must thunder through
  the deep.

With such a horrid clang
As on Mount Sinai rang,
  While the red fire and smouldering clouds out-
   brake :
The aged earth aghast
With terror of that blast,
  Shall from the surface to the centre shake ;

ON THE MORNING

When at the world's last session,
The dreadful Judge in middle air shall spread his
     throne.

And then at last our bliss
Full and perfect is,
    But now begins; for from this happy day
The old dragon under ground
In straiter limits bound,
    Not half so far casts his usurped sway,
And wroth to see his kingdom fail,
Swinges the scaly horror of his folded tail.

The oracles are dumb,
No voice or hideous hum
    Runs through the arched roof in words deceiv-
     ing.
Apollo from his shrine
Can no more divine,
    With hollow shriek the steep of Delphos leaving.
No nightly trance, or breathed spell,
Inspires the pale-eyed priest from the prophetic
    cell.

The lonely mountains o'er,
And the resounding shore,
    A voice of weeping heard and loud lament;
From haunted spring and dale,
Edged with poplar pale,
    The parting Genius is with sighing sent;

58

OF CHRIST'S NATIVITY

With flower-inwoven tresses torn,
The Nymphs in twilight shade of tangled thickets
    mourn.

In consecrated earth
And on the holy hearth
    The Lars and Lemures moan with midnight
        plaint;
In urns and altars round,
A drear and dying sound
    Affrights the Flamens at their service quaint;
And the chill marble seems to sweat,
While each peculiar power foregoes his wonted seat.

Peor and Baälim
Forsake their temples dim,
    With that twice-batter'd god of Palestine;
And mooned Ashtaroth,
Heaven's queen and mother both,
    Now sits not girt with tapers' holy shine;
The Libyc Hammon shrinks his horn,
In vain the Tyrian maids their wounded Thammuz
    mourn.

And sullen Moloch, fled,
Hath left in shadows dread
    His burning idol all of blackest hue;
In vain with cymbals' ring
They call the grisly king,
    In dismal dance about the furnace blue;

ON THE MORNING

The brutish gods of Nile as fast,
Isis, and Orus, and the dog Anubis, haste.

Nor is Osiris seen
In Memphian grove or green,
    Trampling the unshower'd grass with lowings
        loud:
Nor can he be at rest
Within his sacred chest,
    Nought but profoundest hell can be his shroud;
In vain with timbrell'd anthems dark
The sable-stoled sorcerers bear his worshipt ark.

He feels from Judah's land
The dreaded Infant's hand;
    The rays of Bethlehem blind his dusky eyn;
Nor all the gods beside
Longer dare abide,
    Not Typhon huge ending in snaky twine:
Our Babe, to show His Godhead true,
Can in His swaddling bands control the damned
        crew.

So when the sun in bed,
Curtain'd with cloudy red,
    Pillows his chin upon an orient wave,
The flocking shadows pale
Troop to th' infernal jail;
    Each fetter'd ghost slips to his several grave,
And the yellow-skirted Fays
Fly after the night-steeds, leaving their moon-
        loved maze.

OF CHRIST'S NATIVITY

But see the Virgin blest
Hath laid her Babe to rest;
　　Time is our tedious song should here have
　　　　ending:
Heaven's youngest-teemed star
Hath fix'd her polish'd car,
　　Her sleeping Lord with handmaid lamp
　　　　attending:
And all about the courtly stable
Bright-harness'd angels sit in order serviceable.

　　　　　　　　　　　　　　　　John Milton.

A HYMN OF THE NATIVITY

Chorus.—Come we shepherds whose blest sight
Hath met Love's noon in Nature's night,
Come, lift we up our loftier song,
And wake the sun that lies too long.

To all our world of well-stol'n joy,
　　He slept and dreamt of no such thing,
While we found out heaven's fairer eye
　　And kist the cradle of our King;
Tell him he rises now too late,
To show us ought worth looking at.

Tell him we now can show him more
　　Than e'er he showed to mortal sight,
Than he himself e'er saw before,
　　Which to be seen needs not his light.
Tell him, Thyrsis, where th' hast been,
Tell him, Thyrsis, what th' hast seen.

A HYMN OF THE NATIVITY

TIT. Gloomy night embraced the place
Where the noble Infant lay,
The Babe looked up and showed His face;
    In spite of darkness it was day.
It was Thy day, Sweet, and did rise
Not from the East but from Thine eyes.
    Chorus.—It was thy day, Sweet, etc.

THYRS. Winter chid aloud and sent
    The angry North to wage his wars,
The North forgot his fierce intent,
    And left perfumes instead of scars;
By those sweet eyes' persuasive powers,
Where he meant frost he scattered flowers.
    Chorus.—By those sweet eyes, etc.

BOTH. We saw Thee in Thy balmy nest,
    Bright dawn of our eternal day !
We saw Thine eyes break from their East
    And chase the trembling shades away:
We saw Thee and we blest the sight,
We saw thee by thine own sweet light.

TIT. Poor world (said I), what wilt thou do
    To entertain this starry Stranger?
Is this the best thou canst bestow,
    A cold and not too cleanly manger?
Contend, ye powers of heaven and earth,
To fit a bed for this huge birth.
    Chorus.—Contend, ye powers, etc.

62

A HYMN OF THE NATIVITY

THYRS. Proud world (said I), cease your contest,
    And let the mighty Babe alone,
The Phœnix builds the Phœnix' nest,
    Love's architecture is all one.
The Babe whose birth embraves this morn,
Made His own bed ere He was born.
        Chorus.—The Babe whose birth, etc.

TIT. I saw the curl'd drops, soft and slow,
    Come hovering o'er the place's head,
Offering their whitest sheets of snow
    To furnish the fair Infant's bed :
Forbear (said I), be not too bold ;
Your fleece is white, but 'tis too cold.
        Chorus.—Forbear (said I), etc.

THYRS. I saw the obsequious seraphins
    Their rosy fleece of fire bestow ;
For well they now can spare their wings,
    Since heaven itself lies here below :
Well done (said I), but are you sure,
Your down so warm will pass for pure ?
        Chorus.—Well done (said I), etc.

TIT. No, no, your King 's not yet to seek
    Where to repose His royal head.
See, see, how soon, His new-bloom'd cheek,
    Twixt 's mother's breasts is gone to bed :
Sweet choice (said I), no way but so,
Not to lie cold, yet sleep in snow.
        Chorus.—Sweet choice (said I), etc.

A HYMN OF THE NATIVITY

BOTH. We saw Thee in Thy balmy nest,
Bright dawn of our eternal day!
We saw Thine eyes break from Their East
   And chase the trembling shades away;
We saw Thee and we blest the sight,
We saw Thee by Thine own sweet light.
     Chorus.—We saw thee, etc.

Full Chorus.—Welcome all wonder in one sight,
   Eternity shut in a span,
Summer in winter, day in night,
   Heaven in earth and God in man!
Great little One! whose all-embracing birth
Lifts earth to heaven, stoops heaven to earth.

Welcome, though not to gold nor silk,
   To more than Cæsar's birthright is,
Two sister seas of virgin milk,
   With many a rarely-tempered kiss,
That breathes at once both maid and mother,
Warms in the one and cools in the other.

She sings thy tears asleep, and dips
   Her kisses in thy weeping eye;
She spreads the red leaves of thy lips
   That in their buds yet blushing lie:
She 'gainst those mother-diamonds tries
The points of her young eagle's eyes.

Welcome, though not to those gay flies
   Gilded i' the beams of earthly kings,

SATAN'S SIGHT OF THE NATIVITY

Slippery souls in smiling eyes,
   But to poor shepherds' home-spun things ;
Whose wealth's their flock, whose wit to be
Well read in their simplicity.

Yet when young April's husband-showers
   Shall bless the fruitful Maia's bed,
We'll bring the first-born of her flowers
   To kiss Thy feet and crown Thy head :
To Thee, dread Lamb, whose love must keep
The shepherds more than they their sheep.

To Thee, meek Majesty ! soft King
   Of simple graces and sweet loves,
Each of us his lamb will bring,
   Each his pair of silver doves,
Till burnt at last in fire of Thy fair eyes,
Ourselves become our own best sacrifice.

Richard Crashaw.

SATAN'S SIGHT OF THE NATIVITY

Heaven's golden-wingèd herald late he saw
To a poor Galilean virgin sent :
How low the bright youth bowed, and with what
   awe
Immortal flowers to her fair hand present.

SATAN'S SIGHT OF THE NATIVITY

He saw th' old Hebrew's womb neglect the law
Of age and barrenness, and her babe prevent
    His birth by his devotion, who began
    Betimes to be a saint, before a man.

He saw rich nectar thaws release the rigour
Of th' icy north, from frost-bound Atlas' hands
His adamantine fetters fall ; green vigour
Gladding the Scythian rocks, and Libyan sands.
He saw a vernal smile sweetly disfigure
Winter's sad face, and through the flowery lands
    Of fair Engaddi's honey-sweating fountains
    With manna, milk, and balm new broach the
    mountains.

He saw how in that blest day-bearing night
The heaven-rebukèd shades made haste away ;
How bright a dawn of angels with new light
Amazed the midnight world, and made a day
Of which the morning knew not ; mad with spight
He mark'd how the poor shepherds ran to pay
    Their simple tribute to the Babe, whose birth
    Was the great business both of heaven and
    earth.

He saw a threefold sun with rich increase
Make proud the ruby portals of the East,
He saw the temple sacred to sweet peace
Adore her Prince's birth flat on her breast.

66

SATAN'S SIGHT OF THE NATIVITY

He saw the falling idols all confess
A coming Deity.   He saw the nest
    Of poisonous and unnatural loves, earth-nurst,
    Touch'd with the world's true antidote, to
    burst.

He saw heaven blossom with a new-born light,
On which, as on a glorious stranger, gazed
The golden eyes of night, whose beam made bright
The way to Bethlem ; and as boldly blazed
(Nor ask'd leave of the sun) by day as night.
By whom (as heaven's illustrious handmaid) raised
Three kings or, what is more, three wise men went
Westward to find the world's true orient.

    .   .   .   .

That the great angel-blinding light should shrink
His blaze to shine in a poor shepherd's eye,
That the unmeasured God so low should sink
As Pris'ner in a few poor rags to lie,
That from His mother's breast He milk should drink
Who feeds with nectar heaven's fair family,
    That a vile manger His low bed should prove
    Who in a throne of stars thunders above :

That He, whom the sun serves, should faintly peep
Through clouds of infant flesh ; that He the old
Eternal Word should be a Child and weep,
That He who made the fire should fear the cold :

A HYMN FOR THE EPIPHANY

That heaven's high majesty His court should keep
In a clay cottage, by each blast controll'd :
    That glory's self should serve our griefs and
      fears,
    And free Eternity submit to years ;

And further, that the law's eternal Giver
Should bleed in His own law's obedience ;
And to the circumcising knife deliver
Himself, the forfeit of His slave's offence ;
That the unblemish'd Lamb, blessed for ever,
Should take the mark of sin, and pain of sense :—
    These are the knotty riddles, whose dark doubt
    Entangle his lost thoughts past getting out.

A HYMN FOR THE EPIPHANY

[Sung as by the three kings.]

1st KING. Bright Babe ! whose awful beauties
    make
The morn incur a sweet mistake ;
2nd KING. For whom the officious heavens devise
To disinherit the sun's rise ;
3rd KING. Delicately to displace
The day, and plant it fairer in thy face ;
1st KING. O Thou born King of loves !
2nd KING. Of lights !
3rd KING. Of joys !

68

A HYMN FOR THE EPIPHANY

    Chorus.—Look up, sweet Babe, look up and see !
For love of Thee,
Thus far from home,
The East is come
To seek herself in Thy sweet eyes.

1st KING. We who strangely went astray,
Lost in a bright
Meridian night ;
2nd KING. A darkness made of too much day ;
3rd KING. Beckoned from far,
By thy fair star,
Lo, at last have found our way.
    Chorus.—To thee, thou Day of Night ; thou East
      of West !
Lo, we at last have found the way
To thee, the world's great universal East,
The general and indifferent day.

1st KING. All-circling point ! all-centring sphere !
The world's one, round, eternal year :
2nd KING. Whose full and all-unwrinkled face,
Nor sinks nor swells, with time or place ;
3rd KING. But everywhere and every while
Is one consistent solid smile.
1st KING. Not vexed and tost,
2nd KING. 'Twixt spring and frost ;
3rd KING. Nor by alternate shreds of light,
Sordidly shifting hands with shades and night.
    Chorus.—O little All, in Thy embrace,
The world lies warm and likes his place ;

A HYMN FOR THE EPIPHANY

Nor does his full globe fail to be
Kissed on both his cheeks by Thee ;
Time is too narrow for Thy year,
Nor makes the whole world Thy half-sphere.

. . . .

Therefore, to Thee, and Thine auspicious ray,
(Dread sweet !), lo thus,
At least by us,
The delegated eye of day,
Does first his sceptre, then himself, in solemn
        tribute pay :
Thus he undresses
His sacred unshorn tresses ;
At thy adorèd feet thus he lays down,
1st KING. His glorious tire
Of flame and fire,
2nd KING. His glittering robe,
3rd KING.   His sparkling crown,
1st KING. His gold,
2nd KING.   His myrrh,
3rd KING.   His frankincense.
    Chorus.—To which he now has no pretence ;
For being show'd by this day's light, how far
He is from sun, enough to make thy star,
His best ambition now is but to be
Something a brighter shadow, sweet ! of thee.
Or on heaven's azure forehead high to stand,
Thy golden index ; with a duteous hand
Pointing us home to our own Sun,
The world's and his Hyperion.

HYMN FOR CHRISTMAS DAY

[Being a dialogue between three shepherds]

1st. Where is this blessed Babe
    That hath made
All the world so full of joy
    And expectation ;
    That glorious Boy
    That crowns each nation
With a triumphant wreath of blessedness ?

2nd. Where should He be but in the throng,
    And among
His angel ministers, that sing
    And take wing
Just as may echo to His voice,
    And rejoice,
When wing and tongue and all
May so procure their happiness?

3rd. But he hath other waiters now :
    A poor cow,
An ox and mule, stand and behold,
    And wonder
That a stable should enfold
    Him that can thunder.
    Chorus.—O what a gracious God have we,
How good ! how great ! even as our misery.

Jeremy Taylor.

HYMN FOR CHRISTMAS DAY

Awake, my soul, and come away:
   Put on thy best array;
   Lest if thou longer stay
Thou lose some minutes of so blest a day.
       Go run,
And bid good-morrow to the sun;
Welcome his safe return
     To Capricorn,
   And that great morn
   Wherein a God was born,
   Whose story none can tell
But He whose every word's a miracle.

To-day Almightiness grew weak;
The Word itself was mute and could not speak.

That Jacob's star which made the sun
To dazzle if he durst look on,
Now mantled o'er in Bethlehem's night,
Borrowed a star to show him light.
He that begirt each zone,
To whom both poles are one,
Who grasped the zodiac in his hand
And made it move or stand,
Is now by nature man,
By stature but a span;
Eternity is now grown short;
A King is born without a court;

72

THE SHEPHERDS

The water thirsts, the fountain's dry ;
And life, being born, made apt to die.

Chorus.—Then let our praises emulate and vie
  With His humility !
Since He's exiled from skies
  That we might rise,—
From low estate of men
Let's sing Him up again !
Each man wind up his heart
To bear a part
In that angelic choir and show
His glory high as He was low.
Let's sing towards men good-will and charity,
Peace upon earth, glory to God on high !
     Hallelujah ! Hallelujah !

THE SHEPHERDS

Sweet, harmless live[r]s ! on whose holy leisure,
  Waits innocence and pleasure ;
Whose leaders to those pastures and clear springs
  Were patriarchs, saints, and kings ;
How happen'd it that in the dead of night
  You only saw true light,
While Palestine was fast asleep, and lay
  Without one thought of day ?

73

THE SHEPHERDS

Was it because those first and blessèd swains
    Were pilgrims on those plains
When they received the promise, for which now
    'Twas there first shown to you?
'Tis true he loves that dust whereon they go
    That serve him here below,
And therefore might for memory of those
    His love there first disclose;
But wretched Salem, once his love, must now
    No voice nor vision know;
Her stately piles with all their height and pride
    Now languishèd and died,
And Bethlem's humble cots above them stept
    While all her seers slept;
Her cedar, fir, hewed stones, and gold were all
    Polluted through their fall;
And those once sacred mansions were now
    Mere emptiness and show.
This made the angel call at reeds and thatch,
    Yet where the shepherds watch,
And God's own lodging, though he could not lack,
    To be a common rack.
No costly pride, no soft-clothed luxury
    In those thin cells could lie;
Each stirring wind and storm blew through their
      cots,
    Which never harboured plots;
Only content and love and humble joys
    Lived there without all noise;
Perhaps some harmless cares for the next day
    Did in their bosoms play,

CHRIST'S NATIVITY

As where to lead their sheep, what silent nook,
  What springs or shades to look ;
But that was all ; and now with gladsome care
  They for the town prepare ;
They leave their flock, and in a busy talk
  All towards Bethlem walk,
To seek their soul's great Shepherd, who was come
  To bring all stragglers home;
Where now they find Him out, and, taught before,
  That Lamb of God adore,
That Lamb, whose days great kings and prophets
    wished
  And longed to see, but missed.
The first light they beheld was bright and gay,
  And turned their night to day;
But to this later light they saw in Him
  Their day was dark and dim.

Henry Vaughan.

CHRIST'S NATIVITY

Awake, glad heart ! get up and sing !
It is the Birthday of thy King.
    Awake ! awake !
    The sun doth shake
Light from his locks, and, all the way
Breathing perfumes, doth spice the day.

Awake ! awake ! hark how th' wood rings,
Winds whisper, and the busy springs

CHRIST'S NATIVITY

A concert make!
Awake! awake!
Man is their high-priest, and should rise
To offer up the sacrifice.

I would I were a bird or star,
Fluttering in woods, or lifted far
Above this inn,
And road of sin!
Then either star or bird should be
Shining or singing still to Thee.

I would I had in my best part
Fit rooms for Thee! or that my heart
Were so clean as
Thy manger was!
But I am all filth, and obscene:
Yet, if thou wilt, Thou canst make clean.

Sweet Jesu! will then.   Let no more
This leper haunt and soil thy door!
Cure him, ease him,
O release him!
And let once more, by mystic birth,
The Lord of life be born in earth.

THE SHEPHERDS' SONG

Sweet music, sweeter far
    Than any song is sweet :
Sweet music, heavenly rare,
    Mine ears, O peers, doth greet.
You gentle flocks, whose fleeces pearled with dew,
  Resemble heaven, whom golden drops make
      bright,
Listen, O listen, now, O not to you
  Our pipes make sport to shorten weary night :
    But voices most divine
      Make blissful harmony :
    Voices that seem to shine,
      For what else clears the sky ?
Tunes can we hear, but not the singers see,
The tunes divine, and so the singers be.

Lo, how the firmament
    Within an azure fold
The flock of stars hath pent,
    That we might them behold,
Yet from their beams proceedeth not this light,
  Nor can their crystals such reflection give.
What then doth make the element so bright ?
  The heavens are come down upon earth to live.

THE SHEPHERDS' SONG

But hearken to the song,
   Glory to glory's King,
And peace all men among,
   These quiristers do sing.
Angels they are, as also (shepherds) He
Whom in our fear we do admire to see.

Let not amazement blind
   Your souls, said he, annoy:
To you and all mankind
   My message bringeth joy.
For lo! the world's great Shepherd now is born,
  A blessed Babe, an Infant full of power:
After long night uprisen is the morn,
  Renowning Bethlem in the Saviour.
   Sprung is the perfect day,
     By prophets seen afar:
   Sprung is the mirthful May,
     Which winter cannot mar.
In David's city doth this Sun appear
Clouded in flesh, yet, shepherds, sit we here?

Edmund Bolton.

AND THEY LAID HIM IN A MANGER

Happy crib, that wert alone
To my God, bed, cradle, throne!
Whilst thy glorious vileness I
View with divine fancy's eye,
Sordid filth seems all the cost,
State, and splendour, crowns do boast.

THEY LAID HIM IN A MANGER

See heaven's sacred majesty
Humbled beneath poverty ;
Swaddled up in homely rags,
On a bed of straw and flags !
He whose hands the heavens display'd,
And the world's foundations laid,
From the world almost exiled,
Of all ornaments despoil'd.
Perfumes bathe him not, new-born,
Persian mantles not adorn ;
Nor do the rich roofs look bright,
With the jasper's orient light.
Where, O royal Infant, be
Th' ensigns of Thy majesty ;
Thy Sire's equalising state ;
And Thy sceptre that rules fate ?
Where 's Thy angel-guarded throne,
Whence Thy laws Thou didst make known—
Laws which heaven, earth, hell obey'd ?
These, ah ! these aside he laid ;
Would the emblem be—of pride
By humility outvied ?

Sir Edward Sherburne.

AT THE SIGN OF THE HEART

But art Thou come, dear Saviour ? hath Thy love
Thus made Thee stoop, and leave Thy throne above

Thy lofty heavens, and thus thyself to dress
In dust to visit mortals ? Could no less

AT THE SIGN OF THE HEART

A condescension serve? and after all
The mean reception of a cratch and stall?

Dear Lord, I'll fetch Thee thence! I have a room
('Tis poor, but 'tis my best) if Thou wilt come

Within so small a cell, where I would fain
Mine and the world's Redeemer entertain,

I mean, my Heart: 'tis sluttish, I confess,
And will not mend Thy lodging, Lord, unless

Thou send before Thy harbinger, I mean
Thy pure and purging Grace, to make it clean

And sweep its nasty corners; then I'll try
To wash it also with a weeping eye.

And when 'tis swept and wash'd, I then will go
And, with Thy leave, I'll fetch some flowers that
   grow

In Thine own garden, Faith and Love, to Thee;
With these I'll dress it up, and these shall be

My rosemary and bays.   Yet when my best
Is done, the room's not fit for such a Guest.

But here's the cure; Thy presence, Lord, alone
Will make a stall a Court, a cratch a Throne.

Anon.

LODGED in an inn
What Guest divine
There meekly lay,
The God of night and day!
In tax-time to pay sums
  He comes,

AT THE SIGN OF THE HEART

Ev'n man's price full:
From Satan's rule
He will set free
Our poor humanity.

To us betake
Blest God! and make
Within our breast
Thy lodging-place and rest;
Thou Temples seek'st, not Inns:
Let sins
No more intrude
On th' Inmate God,
Nor e'er deface
The ornaments of grace.

YET if his majesty our sovereign Lord
Should of his own accord
Friendly himself invite,
And say, 'I'll be your guest to-morrow night,'
How should we stir ourselves, call and command
All hands to work! 'Let no man idle stand.
Set me fine Spanish tables in the hall,
See they be fitted all;
Let there be room to eat,
And order taken that there want no meat.
See every sconce and candlestick made bright,
That without tapers they may give a light.
Look to the presence: are the carpets spread,
The daïs o'er the head,

AT THE SIGN OF THE HEART

The cushions in the chairs,
And all the candles lighted on the stairs?
Perfume the chambers, and in any case
Let each man give attendance in his place.'
Thus if the king were coming would we do,
And 'twere good reason too;
For 'tis a duteous thing
To show all honour to an earthly king,
And after all our travail and our cost,
So he be pleased, to think no labour lost.
But at the coming of the King of heaven,
All's set at six and seven.
We wallow in our sin,
Christ cannot find a chamber in the inn,
We entertain Him always like a stranger,
And as at first still lodge Him in the manger.

AND art Thou come, blest Babe, and come to me?
Come down to teach me how to come to Thee?

Welcome, thrice welcome to my panting soul,
Which, as it loves, doth grieve that 'tis so foul.

The less 'tis fit for Thee come from above,
The more it needs Thee, and the more I love.

SONG OF THE ANGELS AT THE NATIVITY

While shepherds watch'd their flocks by night,
  All seated on the ground,
The Angel of the Lord came down,
  And glory shone around.

SONG OF THE ANGELS AT THE NATIVITY

'Fear not,' said he (for mighty dread
   Had seized their troubled mind) ;
'Glad tidings of great joy I bring
   To you and all mankind.

'To you in David's town this day
   Is born of David's line
The Saviour, who is Christ the Lord ;
   And this shall be the sign :—

'The heavenly Babe you there shall find
   To human view display'd,
All meanly wrapt in swathing-bands,
   And in a manger laid.'

Thus spake the seraph ; and forthwith
   Appear'd a shining throng
Of angels praising God, and thus
   Address'd their joyful song :—

'All glory be to God on high,
   And to the earth be peace ;
Good-will henceforth from heaven to men
   Begin, and never cease !'

                      Nahum Tate.

'SHEPHERDS, rejoice, lift up your eyes,
   And send your fears away ;
News from the region of the skies !
   Salvation 's born to-day.

SONG OF THE ANGELS AT THE NATIVITY

' Jesus, the God whom angels fear,
   Comes down to dwell with you ;
To-day He makes His entrance here,
   But not as monarchs do.

' No gold, nor purple swaddling-bands,
   Nor royal shining things ;
A manger for His cradle stands
   And holds the King of kings.

' Go, shepherds, where the Infant lies,
   And see His humble throne:—
With tears of joy in all your eyes
   Go, shepherds, kiss the Son.'

Thus Gabriel sang : and straight around
   The heavenly armies throng ;
They tune their harps to lofty sound,
   And thus conclude the song :

' Glory to God that reigns above,
   Let peace surround the earth ;
Mortals shall know their Maker's love,
   At their Redeemer's birth.'

Lord ! and shall angels have their songs,
   And men no tunes to raise ?
O may we lose these useless tongues
   When they forget to praise !

A CRADLE SONG

Glory to God that reigns above,
   That pitied us forlorn !
We join to sing our Maker's love—
   For there's a Saviour born.

Dr. Isaac Watts.

A CRADLE SONG

Hush, my dear, lie still and slumber,
   Holy angels guard thy bed !
Heavenly blessings without number
   Gently falling on thy head.

Sleep, my babe; thy food and raiment,
   House and home thy friends provide;
All without thy care or payment
   All thy wants are well supplied.

How much better thou 'rt attended
   Than the Son of God could be,
When from heaven He descended,
   And became a Child like thee !

Soft and easy is thy cradle;
   Coarse and hard thy Saviour lay:
When His birthplace was a stable,
   And His softest bed was hay.

A HYMN FOR CHRISTMAS DAY

See the kinder shepherds round Him,
  Telling wonders from the sky!
Where they sought Him, there they found Him,
  With the virgin-mother by.

See the lovely Babe a-dressing;
  Lovely Infant, how He smiled!
When He wept, the mother's blessing
  Soothed and hushed the holy Child.

Lo, He slumbers in His manger
  Where the hornèd oxen fed;
—Peace, my darling, here's no danger;
  Here's no ox a-near thy bed.

Mayst thou live to know and fear Him
  Trust and love Him all thy days;
Then go dwell for ever near Him,
  See His face, and sing His praise.

I could give thee thousand kisses,
  Hoping what I most desire;
Not a mother's fondest wishes
  Can to greater joys aspire.

A HYMN FOR CHRISTMAS DAY

Christians, awake, salute the happy morn
Whereon the Saviour of the world was born;
Rise to adore the Mystery of love,
Which hosts of angels chanted from above:

A HYMN FOR CHRISTMAS DAY

With them the joyful tidings first begun
Of God incarnate, and the virgin's Son:
Then to the watchful shepherds it was told,
Who heard th' Angelic Herald's voice—'Behold!
I bring good tidings of a Saviour's birth
To you, and all the nations upon earth;
This day hath God fulfill'd his promised word;
This day is born a Saviour, Christ, the Lord:
In David's city, shepherds, ye shall find
The long-foretold Redeemer of mankind,
Wrapt up in swaddling-clothes, the Babe divine
Lies in a manger; this shall be the sign.'

John Byrom.

A HYMN FOR CHRISTMAS DAY

Hark, the glad sound! the Saviour comes,
  The Saviour promised long;
Let every heart prepare a throne,
  And every voice a song!

He comes, the prisoners to release
  In Satan's bondage held;
The gates of brass before Him burst,
  The iron fetters yield.

He comes, the broken heart to bind,
  The bleeding soul to cure,
And with the treasures of His grace
  T' enrich the humble poor.

A HYMN FOR CHRISTMAS DAY

Our glad Hosannas, Prince of Peace,
  Thy welcome shall proclaim,
And heaven's eternal arches ring
  With Thy belovèd name.

Philip Doddridge.

A HYMN FOR CHRISTMAS DAY

Hark! how all the welkin rings,
Glory to the King of kings!
Peace on earth, and mercy mild,
God and sinners reconciled!
Joyful, all ye nations, rise,
Join the triumph of the skies;
Universal nature say,
Christ the Lord is born to-day.

Christ, by highest Heaven adored;
Christ, the Everlasting Lord;
Late in time behold Him come,
Offspring of a Virgin's womb;
Veil'd in flesh the Godhead see;
Hail, th' Incarnate Deity!
Pleased as man with men t' appear,
Jesus, our Immanuel here!

Hail! the heavenly Prince of Peace!
Hail! the Sun of Righteousness!
Light and life to all He brings,
Risen with healing in His wings.

88

SHEPHERDS WENT THEIR HASTY WAY

Mild He lays His glory by,
Born that man no more may die,
Born to raise the sons of earth,
Born to give them second birth.

Charles Wesley.

THE SHEPHERDS WENT THEIR HASTY WAY.

The shepherds went their hasty way,
  And found the lowly stable-shed,
Where the virgin-mother lay;
  And now they checked their eager tread,
For to the Babe that at her bosom clung,
A mother's song the virgin-mother sung.

They told her how a glorious light,
  Streaming from a heavenly throng,
Around them shone, suspending night!
  While sweeter than a mother's song,
Blest angels heralded the Saviour's birth,
Glory to God on high! and peace on earth!

She listened to the tale divine,
  And closer still the Babe she prest;
And while she cried, The Babe is mine!
  The milk rushed faster to her breast:
Joy rose within her like a summer's morn;
Peace, peace on earth! the Prince of Peace is born.

SHEPHERDS WENT THEIR HASTY WAY

Thou mother of the Prince of Peace,
  Poor, simple, and of low estate!
That strife should vanish, battle cease,
  O why should this thy soul elate?
Sweet music's loudest note, the poet's story,—
Didst thou ne'er love to hear of fame and glory?

And is not War a youthful king,
  A stately hero clad in mail?
Beneath his footsteps laurels spring;
  Him earth's majestic monarchs hail
Their friend, their playmate! and his bold bright
    eye
Compels the maiden's love-confessing sigh.

'Tell this in some more courtly scene,
  To maids and youths in robes of state!
I am a woman poor and mean,
  And therefore is my soul elate:
War is a ruffian all with guilt defiled,
That from the aged father tears his child.

'A murderous fiend by fiends adored,
  He kills the sire and starves the son;
The husband kills and from her board
  Steals all his widow's toil had won;
Plunders God's world of beauty; rends away
All safety from the night, all comfort from the
    day.

90

FROM OTTFRIED'S PARAPHRASE

'Then wisely is my soul elate,
 That strife should vanish, battle cease;
I'm poor and of a low estate,
 The mother of the Prince of Peace.
Joy rises in me, like a summer's morn:
Peace, peace on earth! the Prince of Peace is born.'
                                    Samuel Taylor Coleridge.

FROM OTTFRIED'S PARAPHRASE OF THE GOSPEL

She gave with joy her virgin breast;
She hid it not, she bared the breast
Which suckled that divinest Babe!
Blessed, blessed were the breasts
Which the Saviour Infant kiss'd;
And blessed, blessed was the mother
Who wrapp'd His limbs in swaddling clothes,
Singing placed Him on her lap,
Hung o'er Him with her looks of love,
And soothed Him with a lulling motion.
Blessed! for she shelter'd Him
From the damp and chilling air;
Blessed, blessed! for she lay
With such a Babe in one blest bed,
Close as babes and mothers lie!
Blessed, blessed evermore,
With her virgin lips she kiss'd,
With her arms, and to her breast,
She embraced the Babe divine,
Her Babe divine the virgin-mother!

THE VIRGIN'S CRADLE HYMN

There lives not on this ring of earth
A mortal that can sing her praise.
Mighty mother, virgin pure,
In the darkness and the night
For us she bore the heavenly Lord.

THE VIRGIN'S CRADLE HYMN

Dormi, Jesu! mater ridet
Quæ tam dulcem somnum videt,
   Dormi, Jesu! blandule!
Si non dormis, mater plorat,
Inter fila cantans orat,
Blande, veni, somnule.

Sleep, sweet Babe! my cares beguiling:
Mother sits beside Thee smiling;
   Sleep, my Darling, tenderly;
If Thou sleep not, mother mourneth,
Singing as her wheel she turneth:
   Come, soft slumber, balmily!

BRIGHTEST and best of the sons of the morning!
   Dawn on our darkness, and lend us Thine aid!
Star of the East, the horizon adorning,
   Guide where our Infant Redeemer is laid!

Cold on His cradle the dew-drops are shining;
   Low lies His head with the beasts of the stall;
Angels adore Him, in slumber reclining,
   Maker and Monarch and Saviour of all.

CHRISTMAS CAROL

Say, shall we yield Him, in costly devotion,
   Odours of Edom and offerings divine ?
Gems of the mountain, and pearls of the ocean,
   Myrrh from the forest, or gold from the mine ?

Vainly we offer each ample oblation ;
   Vainly with gifts would His favour secure ;
Richer by far is the heart's adoration ;
   Dearer to God are the prayers of the poor.

Brightest and best of the sons of the morning !
   Dawn on our darkness, and lend us Thine aid !
Star of the East, the horizon adorning,
   Guide where our Infant Redeemer is laid !
                        Bishop Heber.

CHRISTMAS CAROL

O lovely voices of the sky,
   That hymned the Saviour's birth !
Are ye not singing still on high,
   Ye that sang, ' Peace on earth ' ?
To us yet speak the strains
   Wherewith, in days gone by,
Ye blessed the Syrian swains,
   O voices of the sky.

O clear and shining light, whose beams
   That hour heaven's glory shed,
Around the palms, and o'er the streams,
   And on the shepherd's head.

CHRISTMAS CAROL

Be near thro' life and death,
  As in that holiest night,
Of Hope, and Joy, and Faith,
  O clear and shining light!

O star which led to Him whose love
  Brought down man's ransom free,
Where art thou?—'midst the hosts above
  May we still gaze on thee?
In heaven thou art not set,
  Thy rays earth might not dim—
Send them to guide us yet!
  O star which led to Him!

                    Felicia Hemans.

THEY leave the land of gems and gold,
  The shining portals of the East;
For Him, the woman's Seed foretold,
  They leave the revel and the feast.

To earth their sceptres they have cast,
  And crowns by kings ancestral worn;
They track the lonely Syrian waste;
  They kneel before the Babe new born.

O happy eyes that saw Him first;
  O happy lips that kissed His feet;
Earth slakes at last her ancient thirst;
  With Eden's joy her pulses beat.

94

A CHRISTMAS CAROL

True kings are those who thus forsake
  Their kingdoms for the Eternal King;
Serpent, her foot is on thy neck;
  Herod, thou writhest, but canst not sting.

He, He is King, and He alone
  Who lifts that infant hand to bless;
Who makes His mother's knee His throne,
  Yet rules the starry wilderness.

Aubrey de Vere.

A CHRISTMAS CAROL

It chanced upon the merry merry Christmas eve
  I went sighing past the church across the moor-
      land dreary,—
'Oh! never sin and want and woe this earth will
      leave,
  And the bells but mock the wailing round, they
      sing so cheery.
How long, O Lord! how long before Thou come
      again?
  Still in cellar, and in garret, and on moorland
      dreary
The orphans moan, and widows weep, and poor
      men toil in vain,
  Till earth is sick of hope deferred, though
      Christmas bells be cheery.'

CHRISTMAS DAY

Then arose a joyous clamour from the wildfowl on
     the mere,
  Beneath the stars, across the snow, like clear
     bells ringing,
And a voice within cried—'Listen!—Christmas
     carols even here!
  Though thou be dumb, yet o'er their work the
     stars and snows are singing.
Blind! I live, I love, I reign; and all the nations
     through
  With the thunder of My judgments even now are
     ringing;
Do thou fulfil thy work, but as yon wildfowl do,
  Thou wilt hear no less the wailing, yet hear
     through it angels singing.

                         C. Kingsley.

CHRISTMAS DAY—1868

How will it dawn, the coming Christmas Day?
A northern Christmas, such as painters love,
And kinsfolk, shaking hands but once a year,
And dames who tell old legends by the fire?
Red sun, blue sky, white snow, and pearled ice,
Keen ringing air, which sets the blood on fire.
And makes the old man merry with the young,
Through the short sunshine, through the longer
     night?
  Or southern Christmas, dark and dank with mist,
And heavy with the scent of steaming leaves,

96

CHRISTMAS DAY

And rosebuds mouldering on the dripping porch ;
One twilight, without rise or set of sun,
Till beetles drone along the hollow lane,
And round the leafless hawthorns, flitting bats
Hawk the pale moths of winter? Welcome then
At best, the flying gleam, the flying shower,
The rain-pools glittering on the long white roads,
And shadows sweeping on from down to down
Before the salt Atlantic gale : yet come
In whatsoever garb, or gay or sad,
Come fair, come foul, 'twill still be Christmas Day.
　　How will it dawn, the coming Christmas Day?
To sailors lounging on the lonely deck
Beneath the rushing trade-wind? Or to him,
Who by some noisome harbour of the East,
Watches swart arms roll down the precious bales,
Spoils of the tropic forests ; year by year
Amid the din of heathen voices groaning
Himself half heathen? How to those—brave hearts!
Who toil with laden loins and sinking stride,
Beside the bitter wells of treeless sands
Toward the peaks which flood the ancient Nile,
To free a tyrant's captives? How to those—
New patriarchs of the new-found underworld—
Who stand, like Jacob, on the virgin lawns,
And count their flocks' increase? To them that day
Shall dawn in glory, and solstitial blaze
Of full midsummer sun : to them that morn,
Gay flowers beneath their feet, gay birds aloft,
Shall tell of nought but summer : but to them,
Ere yet, unwarned by carol or by chime,

CHRISTMAS DAY

They spring into the saddle, thrills may come
From that great heart of Christendom which beats
Round all the worlds; and gracious thoughts of
    youth;
Of steadfast folk, who worship God at home;
Of wise words, learnt beside their mothers' knee;
Of innocent faces upturned once again,
In awe and joy to listen to the tale,
Of God made man, and in a manger laid:
May soften, purify, and raise the soul
From selfish cares, and growing lust of gain,
And phantoms of this dream which some call life,
Toward the eternal facts; for here or there,
Summer or winter, 'twill be Christmas Day.
    Blest day, which aye reminds us, year by year,
What 'tis to be a man: to curb and spurn
The tyrant in us: that ignobler self
Which boasts, not loathes, its likeness to the brute,
And owns no good save ease, no ill save pain,
No purpose, save its share in that wild war
In which, through countless ages, living things
Compete in internecine greed.—Ah God!
Are we as creeping things, which have no Lord?
That we are brutes, great God, we know too well:
Apes daintier-featured: silly birds who flaunt
Their plumes unheeding of the fowler's step;
Spiders, who catch with paper, not with webs,
Tigers, who slay with cannon and sharp steel,
Instead of teeth and claws:—all these we are.
Are we no more than these; and born but to
    compete—

CHRISTMAS DAY

To envy and devour, like beast or herb ;
Mere fools of nature ; puppets of strong lusts,
Taking the sword, to perish with the sword
Upon the universal battle-field,
Even as the things upon the moor outside ?
   The heath eats up green grass and delicate
    flowers,
The pine eats up the heath, the grub the pine,
The finch the grub, the hawk the silly finch ;
And man, the mightiest of all beasts of prey,
Eats what he lists ; the strong eat up the weak,
The many eat the few ; great nations, small ;
And he who cometh in the name of all—
He, greediest, triumphs by the greed of all ;
And, armed by his own victims, eats up all :
While ever out of the eternal heavens
Looks patient down the great magnanimous
    God,
Who, Maker of all worlds, did sacrifice
All to Himself ! Nay, but Himself to one :
Who taught mankind on that first Christmas Day
What 'twas to be a man ; to give, not take ;
To serve, not rule ; to nourish, not devour ;
To help, not crush ; if need, to die, not live.
   Oh blessed day, which giv'st the eternal lie
To self, and sense, and all the brute within ;
Oh, come to us, amid this war of life ;
To hall and hovel, come ; to all who toil
In senate, shop, or study ; and to those
Who, sundered by the wastes of half a world,
Ill-warned, and sorely tempted, ever face

HYMN FOR THE NATIVITY

Nature's brute powers, and men unmanned to
    brutes.
Come to them, blest and blessing, Christmas Day.
Tell them once more the tale of Bethlehem ;
The kneeling shepherds, and the Babe Divine:
And keep them men indeed, fair Christmas Day.

HYMN FOR THE NATIVITY

Happy night and happy silence downward softly
    stealing,
  Softly stealing over land and sea,
Stars from golden censers swing a silent eager
    feeling
  Down on Judah, down on Galilee ;
And all the wistful air, and earth, and sky,
Listened, listened for the gladness of a cry.

Holy night, a sudden flash of light its way is
    winging :
  Angels, angels, all above, around ;
Hark, the angel voices, hark, the angel voices
    singing ;
  And the sheep are lying on the ground.
Lo, all the wistful air, and earth, and sky,
Listen, listen to the gladness of the cry.

Happy night at Bethlehem ; soft little hands are
    feeling,
  Feeling in the manger with the kine :

100

HYMN FOR THE NATIVITY

Little hands, and eyelids closed in sleep, while
    angels kneeling,
  Mary mother, hymn the Babe Divine.
Lo, all the wistful air, and earth, and sky,
Listen, listen to the gladness of the cry.

Wide, as if the light were music, flashes adoration:
  'Glory be to God, nor ever cease.'
All the silence thrills, and speeds the message of
    salvation:
  'Peace on earth, good-will to men of peace.'
Lo, all the wistful air, and earth, and sky,
Listen, listen to the gladness of the cry.

Holy night, thy solemn silence evermore enfoldeth
  Angel songs and peace from God on high:
Holy night, thy watcher still with faithful eye
    beholdeth
  Wings that wave, and angel glory nigh.
Lo, hushed is strife in air, and earth, and sky,
Still thy watchers hear the gladness of the cry.

Praise Him, ye who watch the night, the silent
    night of ages:
  Praise Him, shepherds, praise the Holy Child;
Praise Him, ye who hear the light, O praise Him,
    all ye sages;
  Praise Him children, praise Him meek and mild.
Lo, peace on Earth, glory to God on high,
Listen, listen to the gladness of the cry.

Edward Thring.

A CHRISTMAS CAROL

In the bleak mid-winter
  Frosty winds made moan,
Earth stood hard as iron,
  Water like a stone;
Snow had fallen, snow on snow,
  Snow on snow,
In the bleak mid-winter
  Long ago.

Our God, heaven cannot hold Him,
  Nor earth sustain;
Heaven and earth shall flee away
  When He comes to reign:
In the bleak mid-winter
  A stable-place sufficed
The Lord God Almighty
  Jesus Christ.

Enough for him whom cherubim
  Worship night and day,
A breastful of milk
  And a mangerful of hay;
Enough for him whom angels
  Fall down before,
The ox and ass and camel
  Which adore.

MASTERS, IN THIS HALL

Angels and archangels
  May have gathered there.
Cherubim and seraphim
  Thronged the air :
But only His mother,
  In her maiden bliss,
Worshipped the Beloved
  With a kiss.

What can I give Him,
  Poor as I am ?
If I were a shepherd
  I would bring a lamb,
If I were a wise man
  I would do my part,—
Yet what I can I give Him :
  Give my heart.

Christina Rossetti.

MASTERS, IN THIS HALL

To Bethlem did they go, the shepherds three ;
To Bethlem did they go, to see whe'r it were so or no,
  Whether Christ were born or no
    To set men free.

Masters, in this hall,
  Hear ye news to-day

MASTERS, IN THIS HALL

Brought over sea,
  And ever I you pray,
    Nowell! Nowell! Nowell! Nowell!
      Sing we clear!
    Holpen are all folk on earth,
      Born is God's Son so dear.

Going over the hills
  Through the milk-white snow,
Heard I ewes bleat
  While the wind did blow.
    Nowell, etc.

Shepherds many an one
  Sat among the sheep;
No man spake more word
  Than they had been asleep.
    Nowell, etc.

Quoth I, 'Fellows mine,
  Why this guise sit ye?
Making but dull cheer,
  Shepherds though ye be?
    Nowell, etc.

'Shepherds should of right
  Leap and dance and sing;
Thus to see ye sit
  Is a right strange thing.'
    Nowell, etc.

104

MASTERS, IN THIS HALL

Quoth these fellows then,
  'To Bethlem town we go,
To see a mighty Lord
  Lie in a manger low.'
    Nowell, etc.

'How name ye this Lord,
  Shepherds?' then said I.
'Very God,' they said,
  'Come from heaven high.'
    Nowell, etc.

Then to Bethlem town
  We went two and two,
And in a sorry place
  Heard the oxen low.
    Nowell, etc.

Therein did we see
  A sweet and goodly May,
And a fair old man ;
  Upon the straw she lay.
    Nowell, etc.

And a little Child
  On her arm had she ;
'Wot ye who this is ?'
  Said the hinds to me.
    Nowell, etc.

MASTERS, IN THIS HALL

Ox and ass Him know,
   Kneeling on their knee :
Wondrous joy had I
   This little Babe to see.
      Nowell, etc.

This is Christ the Lord,
   Masters, be ye glad !
Christmas is come in,
   And no folk should be sad.
      Nowell, etc.

William Morris.

OUTLANDERS, WHENCE COME YE LAST ?

Outlanders, whence come ye last ?
   The snow in the street and the wind on the door.
Through what green sea and great have ye past ?
   Minstrels and maids, stand forth on the floor.

From far away, O masters mine,
   The snow in the street and the wind on the door.
We come to bear you goodly wine :
   Minstrels and maids, stand forth on the floor.

From far away we come to you,
   The snow in the street and the wind on the door.
To tell of great tidings strange and true :
   Minstrels and maids, stand forth on the floor.

OUTLANDERS, WHENCE COME YE LAST?

News, news of the Trinity,
  The snow in the street and the wind on the door.
And Mary and Joseph from over the sea:
  Minstrels and maids, stand forth on the floor.

For as we wandered far and wide,
  The snow in the street and the wind on the door.
What hap do ye deem there should us betide?
  Minstrels and maids, stand forth on the floor.

Under a bent when the night was deep,
  The snow in the street and the wind on the door.
There lay three shepherds tending their sheep:
  Minstrels and maids, stand forth on the floor.

'O ye shepherds, what have ye seen,
  The snow in the street and the wind on the door,
To slay your sorrow and heal your teen?'
  Minstrels and maids, stand forth on the floor.

'In an ox-stall this night we saw,
  The snow in the street and the wind on the door,
A Babe and a maid without a flaw.'
  Minstrels and maids, stand forth on the floor.

'There was an old man there beside,
  The snow in the street and the wind on the door,
His hair was white and his hood was wide.
  Minstrels and maids, stand forth on the floor.

107

OUTLANDERS, WHENCE COME YE LAST?

'And as we gazed this thing upon,
  The snow in the street and the wind on the door,
Those twain knelt down to the Little One.
  Minstrels and maids, stand forth on the floor.

'And a marvellous song we straight did hear,
  The snow in the street and the wind on the door,
That slew our sorrow and healed our care.'
  Minstrels and maids, stand forth on the floor.

News of a fair and marvellous thing,
  The snow in the street and the wind on the door.
Nowell, nowell, nowell, we sing!
  Minstrels and maids, stand forth on the floor.

SIR GALAHAD, A CHRISTMAS MYSTERY

It is the longest night in all the year,
  Near on the day when the Lord Christ was
      born;
Six hours ago I came and sat down here,
  And ponder'd sadly, wearied and forlorn.

The winter wind that pass'd the chapel door,
  Sang out a moody tune, that went right well
With mine own thoughts: I look'd down on the
      floor,
  Between my feet, until I heard a bell

108

SIR GALAHAD, A CHRISTMAS MYSTERY

Sound a long way off through the forest deep,
  And toll on steadily; a drowsiness
Came on me, so that I fell half asleep,
  As I sat there not moving: less and less

I saw the melted snow that hung in beads
  Upon my steel shoes; less and less I saw
Between the tiles the bunches of small weeds:
  Heartless and stupid, with no touch of awe

Upon me, half shut eyes upon the ground
  I thought; O Galahad! the days go by,
Stop and cast up now that which you have found,
  So sorely you have wrought and painfully.

Night after night your horse treads down alone
  The sere damp fern, night after night you sit
Holding the bridle like a man of stone,
  Dismal, unfriended, what thing comes of it.

And what if Palomydes also ride,
  And over many a mountain and bare heath
Follow the questing beast with none beside?
  Is he not able still to hold his breath

With thoughts of Iseult? doth he not grow pale
  With weary striving to seem best of all
To her, 'as she is best,' he saith? to fail
  Is nothing to him, he can never fall.

SIR GALAHAD, A CHRISTMAS MYSTERY

For unto such a man love-sorrow is
   So dear a thing unto his constant heart,
That even if he never win one kiss,
   Or touch from Iseult, it will never part.

And he will never know her to be worse
   Than in his happiest dreams he thinks she is:
Good knight, and faithful, you have 'scaped the curse
   In wonderful-wise; you have great store of bliss.

Yea, what if Father Launcelot ride out,
   Can he not think of Guenevere's arms, round
Warm and lithe about his neck, and shout
   Till all the place grows joyful with the sound?

And when he lists can often see her face,
   And think, 'Next month I kiss you, or next week,
And still you think of me': therefore the place
   Grows very pleasant, whatsoever he seek.

But me, who ride alone, some carle shall find
   Dead in my arms in the half-melted snow,
When all unkindly with the shifting wind,
   The thaw comes on at Candlemas: I know

Indeed that they will say: 'This Galahad
   If he had lived had been a right good knight;
Ah! poor chaste body!' but they will be glad,
   Not most alone, but all, when in their sight

SIR GALAHAD, A CHRISTMAS MYSTERY

That very evening in their scarlet sleeves
   The gay-dressed minstrels sing; no maid will talk
Of sitting on my tomb, until the leaves,
   Grown big upon the bushes of the walk,

East of the Palace-pleasaunce, make it hard
   To see the minster therefrom: well-a-day!
Before the trees by autumn were well bared,
   I saw a damozel with gentle play,

Within that very walk say last farewell
   To her dear knight, just riding out to find
(Why should I choke to say it?) the Sangreal,
   And their last kisses sunk into my mind.

Yea, for she stood lean'd forward on his breast,
   Rather, scarce stood; the back of one dear hand,
That it might well be kiss'd, she held and press'd
   Against his lips; long time they stood there,
      fann'd

By gentle gusts of quiet frosty wind,
   Till Mador de la Porte a-going by,
And my own horse-hoofs roused them; they
      untwined,
   And parted like a dream. In this way I,

With sleeply face bent to the chapel floor,
   Kept musing half asleep, till suddenly
A sharp bell rang from close beside the door,
   And I leapt up when something pass'd me by,

SIR GALAHAD, A CHRISTMAS MYSTERY

Shrill ringing going with it, still half blind
   I stagger'd after, a great sense of awe
At every step kept gathering on my mind,
   Thereat I have no marvel, for I saw

One sitting on the altar as a throne,
   Whose face no man could say he did not know,
And though the bell still rang, he sat alone,
   With raiment half blood-red, half white as snow.

Right so I fell upon the floor and knelt,
   Not as one kneels in church when mass is said,
But in a heap, quite nerveless, for I felt
   The first time what a thing was perfect dread.

But mightily the gentle voice came down:
   'Rise up, and look and listen, Galahad,
Good knight of God, for you will see no frown
   Upon my face; I came to make you glad.

'For that you say that you are all alone,
   I will be with you always, and fear not
You are uncared for, though no maiden moan
   Above your empty tomb; for Launcelot,

'He in good time shall be my servant too,
   Meantime, take note whose sword first made
      him knight,
And who has loved him alway, yea, and who
   Still trusts him alway, though in all men's sight,

SIR GALAHAD, A CHRISTMAS MYSTERY

'He is just what you know, O Galahad,
   This love is happy even as you say,
But would you for a little time be glad,
   To make ME sorry long day after day?

'Her warm arms round his neck half throttle me,
   The hot love-tears burn deep like spots of lead,
Yea, and the years pass quick : right dismally
   Will Launcelot at one time hang his head ;

'Yea, old and shrivell'd he shall win my love.
   Poor Palomydes fretting out his soul !
Not always is he able, son, to move
   His love, and do it honour : needs must roll

'The proudest destrier sometimes in the dust,
   And then 'tis weary work ; he strives beside
Seem better than he is, so that his trust
   Is always on what chances may betide ;

'And so he wears away, my servant, too,
   When all these things are gone, and wretchedly
He sits and longs to moan for Iseult, who
   Is no care now to Palomydes : see,

'O good son Galahad, upon this day,
   Now even, all these things are on your side,
But these you fight not for ; look up, I say,
   And see how I can love you, for no pride

SIR GALAHAD, A CHRISTMAS MYSTERY

'Closes your eyes, no vain lust keeps them down.
    See now you have ME always; following
That holy vision, Galahad, go on,
    Until at last you come to me to sing

'In heaven always, and to walk around
    The garden where I am': he ceased, my face
And wretched body fell upon the ground;
    And when I look'd again, the holy place

Was empty; but right so the bell again
    Came to the chapel door, there entered
Two angels first, in white, without a stain,
    And scarlet wings, then after them a bed

Four ladies bore, and set it down beneath
    The very altar-step, and while for fear
I scarcely dared to move or draw my breath,
    Those holy ladies gently came a-near,

And quite unarm'd me, saying: 'Galahad,
    Rest here a while and sleep, and take no thought
Of any other thing than being glad;
    Hither the Sangreal will be shortly brought.

'Yet must you sleep the while it stayeth here.'
    Right so they went away, and I, being weary,
Slept long and dream'd of heaven: the bell comes
        near,
    I doubt it grows to morning.   Miserere!

SIR GALAHAD, A CHRISTMAS MYSTERY

[Enter two angels in white, with scarlet wings;
also, four ladies in gowns of red and green; also
an angel, bearing in his hands a surcoat of white,
with a red cross.]

AN ANGEL

O servant of the high God, Galahad!
  Rise and be arm'd, the Sangreal is gone forth
Through the great forest, and you must be had
  Unto the sea that lieth on the north:

There shall you find the wondrous ship wherein
  The spindles of King Solomon are laid,
And the sword that no man draweth without sin,
  But if he be most pure: and there is stay'd,

Hard by, Sir Launcelot, whom you will meet
  In some short space upon that ship: first, though,
Will come here presently that lady sweet,
  Sister of Percival, whom you well know,

And with her Bors and Percival: stand now,
  These ladies will to arm you.

FIRST LADY [putting on the hauberke]
                        Galahad,
That I may stand so close beneath your brow,
  I, Margaret of Antioch, am glad.

SECOND LADY [girding him with the sword]
That I may stand and touch you with my hand,
  O Galahad, I, Cecily, am glad.

SIR GALAHAD, A CHRISTMAS MYSTERY

THIRD LADY [buckling on the spurs]
That I may kneel while up above you stand,
 And gaze at me, O holy Galahad,

I, Lucy, am most glad.

FOURTH LADY [putting on the basnet]
      O gentle knight,
 That you bow down to us in reverence,
We are most glad, I, Katherine, with delight
 Must needs fall trembling.

ANGEL [putting on the crossed surcoat]
        Galahad, we go hence,

For here, amid the straying of the snow,
 Come Percival's sister, Bors, and Percival.
[The four Ladies carry out the bed, and all go but
Galahad.]

GALAHAD
How still and quiet everything seems now !
 They come, too, for I hear the horsehoofs fall.

[Enter Sir Bors, Sir Percival, and his Sister.]
Fair friends and gentle lady, God you save !
 A many marvels have been here to-night ;
Tell me what news of Launcelot you have,
 And has God's body ever been in sight.

SIR BORS
Why, as for seeing that same holy thing,
 As we were riding slowly side by side,

116

SIR GALAHAD, A CHRISTMAS MYSTERY

An hour ago, we heard a sweet voice sing,
   And through the bare twigs saw a great light
      glide

With many-colour'd raiment, but far off,
   And so pass'd quickly—from the court nought
      good;
Poor merry Dinadan, that with jape and scoff
   Kept us all merry, in a little wood

Was found all hack'd and dead; Sir Lionel
   And Gauwaine have come back from the great
      quest,
Just merely shamed; and Lauvaine, who loved well
   Your father Launcelot, at the king's behest

Went out to seek him, but was almost slain,
   Perhaps is dead now; everywhere
The knights come foil'd from the great quest; in
      vain,
   In vain they struggle for the vision fair.

·Three·Damsels·in·the·Queen's·Chamber·

Three damsels in the queen's chamber,
   The queen's mouth was most fair ;
She spake a word of God's mother,
   As the combs went in her hair.
      Mary that is of might,
      Bring us to thy Son's sight.

They held the gold combs out from her,
   A span's length off her head ;
She sang this song of God's mother,
   And of her bearing-bed.
      Mary, most full of grace,
      Bring us to thy Son's face.
118

THREE DAMSELS IN QUEEN'S CHAMBER

When she sat at Joseph's hand,
  She looked against her side;
And either way from the short silk band
  Her girdle was all wried.
      Mary, that all good may,
      Bring us to thy Son's way.

Mary had three women for her bed,
  The twain were maidens clean;
The first of them had white and red,
  The third had riven green.
      Mary, that is so sweet,
      Bring us to thy Son's feet.

She had three women for her hair,
  Two were gloved soft and shod;
The third had feet and fingers bare,
  She was the likest God.
      Mary, that wieldeth land,
      Bring us to thy Son's hand.

She had three women for her ease,
  The twain were good women;
The first two were the two Maries,
  The third was Magdalen.
      Mary, that perfect is,
      Bring us to thy Son's kiss.

Joseph had three workmen in his stall,
  To serve him well upon;

THREE DAMSELS IN QUEEN'S CHAMBER

The first of them were Peter and Paul,
  The third of them was John.
    Mary, God's handmaiden,
    Bring us to thy Son's ken.

'If your child be none other man's,
  But if it be very mine,
The bed-stead shall be gold two spans,
  The bed-foot silver fine.'
    Mary, that made God mirth,
    Bring us to thy Son's birth.

'If the child be some other man's,
  And if it be none of mine,
The manger shall be straw two spans,
  Betwixen kine and kine.'
    Mary, that made sin cease,
    Bring us to thy Son's peace.

Christ was born upon this wise,
  It fell on such a night,
Neither with sounds of psalteries,
  Nor with fire for light.
    Mary, that is God's spouse,
    Bring us to thy Son's house.

The star came out upon the east,
  With a great sound and sweet:
Kings gave gold to make him feast,
  And myrrh for him to eat.
    Mary, of thy sweet mood,
    Bring us to thy Son's good.

MARY MOTHER OF DIVINE GRACE

He had two handmaids at his head,
   One handmaid at his feet;
The twain of them were fair and red,
   The third one was right sweet.
     Mary, that is most wise,
     Bring us to thy Son's eyes.   Amen.
                   A. C. Swinburne.

MARY MOTHER OF DIVINE GRACE, COMPARED TO THE AIR WE BREATHE

Wild air, world-mothering air,
Nestling me everywhere,
That each eyelash or hair
Girdles; goes home betwixt
The fleeciest, frailest-flixed
Snow-flake; that's fairly mixed
With riddles, and is rife
In every least thing's life;
This needful, never spent
And nursing element;
My more than meat and drink,
My meal at every wink;
This air which by life's law
My lung must draw and draw
Now, but to breathe its praise,—
Minds me in many ways
Of her who not only
Gave God's infinity,
Dwindled to infancy,

MARY MOTHER OF DIVINE GRACE

Welcome in womb and breast,
Birth, milk, and all the rest,
But mothers each new grace
That does now reach our race,
Mary Immaculate,
Merely a woman, yet
Whose presence, power is
Great as no goddess's
Was deemèd, dreamèd; who
This one work has to do—
Let all God's glory through,
God's glory, which would go
Thro' her and from her flow
Off, and no way but so.
 I say that we are wound
With mercy round and round
As if with air: the same
Is Mary, more by name,
She, wild web, wondrous robe,
Mantles the guilty globe.
Since God has let dispense
Her prayers His providence.
Nay, more than almoner,
The sweet alms' self is her
And men are meant to share
Her life as life does air.
 If I have understood,
She holds high motherhood
Towards all our ghostly good,
And plays in grace her part
About man's beating heart,

MARY MOTHER OF DIVINE GRACE

Laying like air's fine flood
The death-dance in his blood;
Yet no part but what will
Be Christ our Saviour still.
Of her flesh he took flesh:
He does take, fresh and fresh,
Though much the mystery how,
Not flesh but spirit now,
And wakes, O marvellous!
New Nazareths in us,
Where she shall yet conceive
Him, morning, noon, and eve;
New Bethlems, and he born
There, evening, noon and morn.
Bethlem or Nazareth,
Men here may draw like breath
More Christ, and baffle death;
Who, born so, comes to be
New self, and nobler me
In each one, and each one
More makes, when all is done,
Both God's and Mary's son.
　　Again, look overhead
How air is azurèd.
O how!　Nay do but stand
Where you can lift your hand
Skywards: rich, rich it laps
Round the four finger-gaps.
Yet such a sapphire-shot
Charged, steepèd sky will not

MARY MOTHER OF DIVINE GRACE

Stain light.   Yea, mark you this:
It does no prejudice.
The glass-blue days are those
When every colour glows,
Each shape and shadow shows.
Blue be it: this blue heaven
The seven or seven times seven
Hued sunbeam will transmit
Perfect, nor alter it.
Or if there does some soft
On things aloof, aloft,
Bloom breathe, that one breath more
Earth is the fairer for.
Whereas did air not make
This bath of blue and slake
This fire, the sun would shake
A blear and blinding ball
With blackness bound, and all
The thick stars round him roll.
Flashing like flecks of coal,
Quartz-fret, or sparks of salt
In grimy vasty vault.
   So God was God of old;
A mother came to mould
Those limbs like ours which are,
What must make our daystar
Much dearer to mankind:
Whose glory bare would blind
Or less would win man's mind.
Through her we may see Him
Made sweeter, not made dim,

124

MARY MOTHER OF DIVINE GRACE

And her hand leaves His light
Sifted to suit our sight.
  Be thou, then, O thou dear
Mother, my atmosphere;
My happier world wherein
To wend and meet no sin;
Above me, round me lie
Fronting my froward eye
With sweet and scarless sky;
Stir in my ears, speak there
Of God's love, O live air,
Of patience, penance, prayer;
World-mothering air, air wild,
Wound with thee, in thee isled,
Fold home, fast fold thy child.

Gerard Hopkins.

The · Three · Kings

THE THREE KINGS

THE THREE KINGS

Three Kings went riding from the East,
  Through fine weather and wet;
'And whither shall we ride,' they said,
  'Where we have not ridden yet?'

'And whither shall we ride,' they said,
  'To find the hidden thing
That turns the course of all our stars
  And all our auguring?'

They were the Wise Men of the East,
  And none so wise as they;
'Alas,' the King of Persia cried,
  'And must ye ride away?

'Yet since ye go a-riding, sirs,
  I pray ye, ride for me;
And carry me my golden gifts,
  To the King o' Galilee.

'Go riding into Palestine
  A long ride and a fair!'
''Tis well!' the Magi answered him,
  'As well as anywhere!'

They rode by day, they rode by night,
  The stars came out on high—

THE THREE KINGS

'And oh!' the King Balthazzar said,
  As he gazed into the sky,

'We ride by day, we ride by night,
  To a King in Galilee,
We leave a King in Persia
  And Kings no less are we.

'Yet often in the deep blue night,
  When stars burn far and dim,
I wish I knew a greater King,
  To fall and worship him.

'A King who should not care to reign
  But wonderful and fair;
A King—a King that were a star,
  Aloft in miles of air!'

'A star is good,' said Melchior,
  'A high unworldly thing;
But I would choose a soul alive
  To be my Lord and King.

'Not Herod, nay, nor Cyrus, nay,
  Not any King at all;
For I would choose a sinless child,
  Laid in a manger stall.'

''Tis well!' the black King Caspar cried,
  'For mighty men are ye;
But no such humble King were meet
  For my simplicity.

THE THREE KINGS

'A star is small and very far,
  A babe's a simple thing:
The very Son of God Himself,
  Shall be my Lord and King!'

The King Balthazzar sighed and smiled;
  'A good youth,' Melchior cried;
And young and old, without a word,
  Along the hills they ride.

Till lo! among the western skies
  There grows a shining thing—
'The Star! Behold the star,' they shout,
  'Behold Balthazzar's King!'

And lo! within the western skies,
  The star begins to flit;
The three Kings spur their horses on
  And follow after it.

And when they reach the King's castle,
  They cry, 'Behold the place!'
But like a shining bird, the star
  Flits on in heaven apace.

Oh, they rode on, and on they rode,
  Till they reached a lonely wold,
Where shepherds keep their flocks by night,
  And the night was chill and cold.

THE THREE KINGS

Oh, they rode on, and on they rode,
  Till they reach a little town,
And there the star in heaven stands still
  Above a stable brown.

The town is hardly a village street,
  The stables old and poor,
But there the star in heaven stands still
  Above the stable door.

And through the open door, the straw
  And the tired beasts they see;
And the Babe, laid in a manger
  That sleepeth peacefully.

'All hail! the King of Melchior!'
  The three Wise Men begin;
King Melchior swings from off his horse,
  And he would have entered in.

But why do the horses whinny and neigh?
  And what thing fills the night
With angels in a wheeling spire
  And streams of heavenly light?

King Melchior kneels upon the grass
  And falls a-praying there;
Balthazzar lets the bridle drop
  And gazes in the air.

THE PEDLAR

But Caspar gives a happy shout
  And hastens to the stall,
'Now hail,' he cries, 'Thou Son of God
  And Saviour of us all.'

A. Mary F. Robinson.

THE PEDLAR

It's Christmas Eve, and the dogs are a-cold,
And the star's in the sky, and the flock's in the fold.

A pedlar came to the homestead gate
  With his pack and his pike, and weary was he;
He said, 'See wares from heaven to buy you!
  Who will chaffer his heart with me?'

It's Christmas Eve, and the dogs are a-cold,
And the star's in the sky, and the flock's in the fold.

The farmer laughed—'For a quittance from hell
  Here's all I've left of a heart for ye!'
Quoth the goodwife—'For a heavenly mansion
  Take, and you're welcome, my heart in fee!'

It's Christmas Eve, and the dogs are a-cold,
And the star's in the sky, and the flock's in the fold.

The younker bought him a kingly crown,
  The men got glory in bliss to be;
The maids chose harps and golden garments,
  Cried, 'Good e'en!' and 'Good bye!' said he.

A MEDITATION FOR CHRISTMAS DAY

It's Christmas Eve, and the dogs are a-cold,
And the star's in the sky, and the flock's in the fold.

But the youngest of all said never a word,
   Her hand to her flaxen head held she;
Till, just as he passed the door, she whispered,
   'Here's my heart, at a gift for thee!'

It's Christmas Eve, and the dogs are a-cold,
And the star's in the sky, and the flock's in the fold.

It's feasting day, and the feast's in heaven,
   And there are our folk all fair to see:
'Have they left no room for My own little maiden?
   Come, she must sit on the throne with Me!'

It's Christmas Eve, and the dogs are a-cold,
And the star's in the sky;—and the lamb's in the fold!
                       W. G. Collingwood.

A MEDITATION FOR CHRISTMAS DAY

Consider, O my soul, what morn is this!
   Whereon the eternal Lord of all things made
For us, poor mortals, and our endless bliss,
   Came down from heaven; and, in a manger laid,
   The first, rich, offerings of our ransom paid:
Consider, O my soul, what morn is this!

A MORNING SONG FOR CHRISTMAS DAY

Consider what estate of fearful woe
    Had then been ours, had He refused this birth;
From sin to sin tossed vainly to and fro,
    Hell's playthings, o'er a doomed and helpless
        earth!
    Had He from us witheld His priceless worth,
Consider man's estate of fearful woe!

Consider to what joys He bids thee rise,
    Who comes, Himself, life's bitter cup to drain!
Ah! look on this sweet Child, whose innocent eyes,
    Ere all be done, shall close in mortal pain,
    That thou at last Love's Kingdom may'st attain:
Consider to what joys He bids thee rise!

Consider all this wonder, O my soul:
    And in thine inmost shrine make music sweet!
Yea, let the world, from furthest pole to pole,
    Join in thy praises this dread birth to greet!
    Kneeling to kiss thy Saviour's infant feet!
Consider all this wonder, O my soul!

Selwyn Image.

A MORNING SONG FOR CHRISTMAS DAY

[For Music.]

1 Wake, what unusual light doth greet
The early dusk of this our street?
2 It is the Lord! it is the Christ!
That hath the will of God sufficed;

A MORNING SONG FOR CHRISTMAS DAY

That, ere the day is born anew,
Himself is born a Child for you.
    Chorus.—The harp, the viol, and the lute,
To strike a praise unto our God!
Bring here the reeds! bring here the flute!
Wake summer from the winter's sod!
Oh, what a feast of feasts is given
To His poor servants, by the King of Heaven!

3 Where is the Lord?
2   Here is the Lord,
At thine own door. Tis He, the Word;
He, at whose face, the eternal speed
Of orb on orb was changed to song.
Shall he the sound of viols heed,
Whose ears have heard so high a throng?
Shall he regard the citherns strung
To whom the morning stars have sung?
Chorus—Then wake, my heart, and sweep the strings,
The seven in the Lyre of Life!
Instead of lutes, the spirit sings;
With praise its quiet house is rife!
Oh, what a feast of feasts is given
To His poor servants, by the King of Heaven!

4 Who is the Lord?
2   He is the Lord,
That Light of light, that Chief of all!
3 Who is the Lord?
2   He is the Lord,
An outcast lying in a stall;

A CHRISTMAS CAROL

For in the inn no room is left,
While the unworthy feast instead ;
He of all welcome is bereft,
And hath not where to lay his head.
1 What fitter place could I prepare,
What better cradle, say, is there
Than this my heart, if that were fair ?
2 Thou hast divined ! A nobler part
In man or angel, or of earth, or skies,
There is not, than a broken heart ;
The which thy God may ne'er despise.

THE HYMN

Chorus—Lord, in my heart a little child,
Now that the snows beat far and wide,
While ever wails the tempest wild,
              Good Lord abide.
Nor go Thou if the summer comes,
Nor if the summer days depart ;
But chiefly make Thy home of homes,
              Lord, in my heart.
                  Herbert P. Horne.

A CHRISTMAS CAROL

In days of old the happy shepherds heard
The angels herald the Eternal Word :
Our ears are dull, such songs avail not now ;
Only the wise beside the manger bow,

A CHRISTMAS CAROL

To fools in vain the whole creation's voice
May sing of God and bid the world rejoice.

The shepherds listened, and one lowly maid
Had seen the Archangel and was not afraid:
O happy Mary! secret bliss was hers—
Flowers breathed of God, birds were His
    choristers;—
Still to the pure in heart each earthly place
May shadow forth some vision of His grace.

Have we no carols? Are we deaf and dumb
Save to the great world's money-murmuring hum?
Does God seem absent? Are the angels gone?
The Unseen is here; His choirs unheard sing on;
And when we tremble in some lonely spot,
He longs to bless us though we know Him not.

                        Annie Matheson.

THE night was darker than ever before
    (So dark is sin),
When the Great Love came to the stable door
    And entered in,

And laid Himself in the breath of kine
    And the warmth of hay,
And whispered to the star to shine,
    And to break, the day.

                    Alice Sewell.

136

CHRISTMAS MERRYMAKING

Caput apri defero

Caput apri defero,
Reddens laudes Domino.
The boar's head in hand bring I,
With garlands gay and rosemary ;
I pray you all sing merrily,
         Qui estis in convivio.

The boar's head, I understand,
Is the chief service in this land ;
Look, wherever it be fand,
         Servite cum cantico.

CAPUT APRI DEFERO

Be glad, lords, both more and less,
  For this hath ordained our steward,
To cheer you all this Christmas,
  The boar's head with mustard.

PROFACE,[1] welcome, welcome proface,
This time is born a child of grace,
That for us mankind hath take.
                  Proface.

A king's son and an emperor,
Is comen out of a maiden's tower,
With us to dwell with great honour.
                  Proface.

This holy time of Christës-mass,
All sorrow and sin we should release,
And cast away all heaviness.
                  Proface.

The good lord of this place entere
Saith welcome to all that now appear
Unto such fare as ye find here.
                  Proface.

Well come to this New Year,
And look ye all be of good cheer ;
Our Lord God be at our dinnere.
                  Proface.

---

[1] i.e. proficiat, may it do you good.

CHRISTMAS MERRYMAKING

CHRISTMAS MERRYMAKING

So now is come our joyful'st feast,
　　Let every man be jolly;
Each room with ivy leaves is drest,
　　And every post with holly.
Though some churls at our mirth repine,
Round your foreheads garlands twine;
Drown sorrow in a cup of wine,
　　And let us all be merry.

Now all our neighbours' chimneys smoke,
　　And Christmas logs are burning;
Their ovens they with baked meats choke,
　　And all their spits are turning.
Without the door let sorrow lie;
And, if for cold it hap to die,
We'll bury't in a Christmas pie,
　　And evermore be merry.

Now every lad is wondrous trim,
　　And no man minds his labour;
Our lasses have provided them
　　A bag-pipe and a tabor;
Young men and maids, and girls and boys,
Give life to one another's joys;
And you anon shall by their noise
　　Perceive that they are merry.

Rank misers now do sparing shun;
　　Their hall of music soundeth;

CHRISTMAS MERRYMAKING

And dogs thence with whole shoulders run,
　So all things there aboundeth.
The country folks themselves advance,
For crowdy-mutton's[1] come out of France;
And Jack shall pipe, and Jill shall dance,
　And all the town be merry.

Ned Squash hath fetched his bands from pawn,
　And all his best apparel;
Brisk Ned hath bought a ruff of lawn,
　With droppings of the barrel.
And those that hardly all the year
Had bread to eat or rags to wear,
Will have both clothes and dainty fare,
　And all the day be merry.

Now poor men to the justices
　With capons make their arrants,
And if they hap to fail of these,
　They plague them with their warrants.
But now they feed them with good cheer,
And what they want they take in beer;
For Christmas comes but once a year,
　And then they shall be merry.

Good farmers in the country nurse
　The poor that else were undone;
Sour landlords spend their money worse
　On lust and pride at London.

---

[1] Fiddlers

CHRISTMAS MERRYMAKING

There the roysters they do play,
Drab and dice their lands away,
Which may be ours another day;
  And therefore let's be merry.

The client now his suit forbears,
  The prisoner's heart is eased;
The debtor drinks away his cares,
  And for the time is pleased.
Though other purses be more fat,
Why should we pine or grieve at that?
Hang sorrow! care will kill a cat,
  And therefore let's be merry.

Hark, how the wags abroad do call
  Each other forth to rambling:
And you'll see them in the hall
  For nuts and apples scrambling.
Hark, how the roofs with laughter sound!
And they'll think the house goes round:
For they the cellar's depth have found,
  And there they will be merry.

The wenches with their wassail-bowls
  About the streets are singing;
The boys are come to catch the owls,
  The wildmare in is bringing.
Our kitchen-boy hath broke his box,
And to the dealing of the ox
Our honest neighbours come by flocks,
  And here they will be merry.

Ceremonies · for · Christmas

CEREMONIES FOR CHRISTMAS

Now kings and queens poor sheep-cotes have,
  And mate with everybody:
The honest now may play the knave,
  And wise men play at noddy.
Some youths will now a-mumming go,
Some others play at Rowland-ho,
And twenty other gameboys mo,
  Because they will be merry.

Then wherefore in these merry days,
  Should we, I pray, be duller?
Ho, let us sing some roundelays,
  To make our mirth the fuller.
And whilst thus inspired we sing,
Let all the streets with echoes ring,
Woods and hills and everything
  Bear witness we are merry.

                           George Wither.

CEREMONIES FOR CHRISTMAS

  Come, bring with a noise,
  My merry, merry boys,
The Christmas log to the firing;
  While my good dame she
  Bids ye all be free,
And drink to your hearts' desiring.

CHRISTMAS EVE

With the last year's brand
Light the new block, and
For good success in his spending,
On your psaltries play,
That sweet luck may
Come while the log is a-teending.[1]

Drink now the strong beer,
Cut the white loaf here ;
The while the meat is a-shredding
For the rare mince-pie,
And the plums stand by
To fill the paste that's a-kneading.

Robert Herrick.

CHRISTMAS EVE: ANOTHER CEREMONY

Come, guard this night the Christmas pie,
That the thief, though ne'er so sly,
With his flesh-hooks don't come nigh
            To catch it

From him, who all alone sits there,
Having his eyes still in his ear
And a deal of nightly fear,
            To watch it.

---

[1] Kindling

146

CHRISTMAS EVE

ANOTHER TO THE MAIDS

Wash your hands, or else the fire
Will not teend to your desire ;
Unwash'd hands, ye maidens, know,
Dead the fire though ye blow.

ANOTHER

Wassail the trees, that they may bear
You many a plum and many a pear ;
For more or less fruits they will bring,
As you do give them wassailing.

THE WASSAIL

Give way, give way, ye gates, and win
An easy blessing to your bin
And basket, by our entering in.

May both with manchet [1] stand replete ;
Your larders too so hung with meat,
That though a thousand, thousand eat,

Yet ere twelve moons shall whirl about
Their silv'ry spheres, then none may doubt
But more 's sent in than was serv'd out.

---

[1] White bread

CHRISTMAS EVE

Next may your dairies prosper so
As that your pans no ebb may know;
But if they do, the more to flow;

Like to a solemn sober stream
Bank'd all with lilies, and the cream
Of sweetest cowslips filling them.

Then, may your plants be prest with fruit,
Nor bee or hive, you have, be mute;
But sweetly sounding like a lute.

Next may your duck and teeming hen
Both to the cock's tread say Amen;
And for their two eggs render ten.

Last may your harrows, shears, and ploughs,
Your stacks, your stocks, your sweetest mows,
All prosper by our virgin vows.

TWELFTH NIGHT

Now, now the mirth comes
With the cake full of plums,
Where bean 's the king of the sport here;
Besides we must know,
The pea also
Must revel as queen in the court here.

148

TWELFTH NIGHT

Begin then to choose
This night as ye use,
Who shall for the present delight here;
Be a king by the lot,
And who shall not
Be Twelfth-day queen for the night here.

Which known, let us make
Joy-sops with the cake;
And let not a man then be seen here,
Who unurg'd will not drink,
To the base from the brink,
A health to the king and the queen here.

Next crown the bowl full
With gentle lamb's wool:
Add sugar, nutmeg, and ginger,
With store of ale too:
And this ye must do
To make the wassail a swindger.

Give then to the king
And queen wassailing:
And though with ale ye be whet here,
Yet part from hence
As free from offence
As when ye innocent met here.

TO SIR SIMON STEWARD

TO SIR SIMON STEWARD

No news of navies burnt at seas ;
No noise of late-spawn'd tittyries ;
No closet plot, or open vent
That frights men with a parliament :
No new device or late-found trick
To read by the stars the kingdom's sick ;
No gin to catch the state, or wring
The free-born nostrils of the king,
We send to you : but here a jolly
Verse crown'd with ivy and with holly,
That tells of winter's tales and mirth,
That milkmaids make about the hearth,
Of Christmas sports, the wassail bowl,
That tost up, after fox-i-th'-hole ;
Of blind-man-buff, and of the care
That young men have to shoe the mare ;
Of twelve-tide cakes, of peas and beans,
Wherewith you make those merry scenes,
Whenas ye choose your king and queen,
And cry out : 'Hey, for our town green' ;
Of ash-heaps in the which ye use
Husbands and wives by streaks to choose ;
Of crackling laurel which foresounds
A plenteous harvest to your grounds :
Of these and such-like things for shift,
We send instead of New Year's gift.
Read then, and when your faces shine
With buxom meat and cap'ring wine,

150

SONG

Remember us in cups full crown'd,
And let our city-health go round,
Quite through the young maids and the men,
To the ninth number, if not ten ;
Until the fired chestnuts leap
For joy to see the fruits ye reap
From the plump chalice and the cup
That tempts till it be tossed up ;
Then as ye sit about your embers,
Call not to mind those fled Decembers,
But think on these that are t' appear
As daughters to the instant year :
Sit crown'd with rosebuds, and carouse
Till Liber Pater twirls the house
About your ears ; and lay upon
The year your cares that 's fled and gone.
And let the russet swains the plough
And harrow hang up resting now ;
And to the bagpipe all address,
Till sleep takes place of weariness.
And thus, throughout, with Christmas plays
Frolic the full twelve holidays.

SONG

Now winter nights enlarge
  The number of their hours ;
And clouds their storms discharge
  Upon the airy towers.

SONG

Let now the chimneys blaze
   And cups o'erflow with wine,
Let well-tuned words amaze
   With harmony divine.
Now yellow waxen lights
   Shall wait on honey love,
While youthful revels, masques, and courtly sights,
   Sleep's leaden spells remove.

This time doth well dispense
   With lovers' long discourse,
Much speech hath some defence,
   Though beauty no remorse.
All do not all things well;
   Some measures comely tread,
Some knotted riddles tell,
   Some poems smoothly read.
The summer hath his joys,
   And winter his delights;
Though love and all his pleasures are but toys,
   They shorten tedious nights.

                  Thomas Campion.

SONG

To shorten winter's sadness,
See where the nymphs with gladness
Disguised all are coming
Right wantonly a-mumming.
           Fa la.

SONG

Whilst youthful sports are lasting
To feasting turn our fasting;
With revels and with wassails
Make grief and care our vassals.
>   Fa la.

For youth it well beseemeth
That pleasure he esteemeth;
And sullen age is hated
That mirth would have abated.
>   Fa la.

>   Anon.

Christmas · Merrymaking

The damsel donned her kirtle sheen;
The hall was dressed with holly green;
Forth to the wood did merry men go
To gather in the mistletoe.
Then opened wide the baron's hall
To vassal, tenant, serf and all;
Power laid his rod of rule aside,
And ceremony doffed his pride.
The heir with roses in his shoes
That night might village partner choose;

CHRISTMAS MERRYMAKING

The lord underogating share
The vulgar game of post-and-pair.
All hailed with uncontrolled delight
And general voice the happy night
That to the cottage as the crown
Brought tidings of salvation down.
The fire with well-dried logs supplied
Went roaring up the chimney wide;
The huge hall-table's oaken face,
Scrubbed till it shone, the day to grace,
Bore then upon its massive board
No mark to part the squire and lord.
Then was brought in the lusty brawn
By old blue-coated serving man;
Then the grim boar's-head frowned on
     high,
Crested with bay and rosemary.
Well can the green-garbed ranger tell
How, when, and where the monster fell,
What dogs before his death be tore,
And all the baiting of the boar.
The wassail round, in good brown bowls,
Garnished with ribbons blithely trowls.
There the huge sirloin reeked; hard by
Plum-porridge stood and Christmas pie;
Nor failed old Scotland to produce
At such high-tide her savoury goose.
Then came the merry masquers in
And carols roared with blithesome din;
If unmelodious was the song
It was a hearty note and strong.

CHRISTMAS MERRYMAKING

Who lists may in their mumming see
Traces of ancient mystery;
White shirts supplied the masquerade,
And smutted cheeks the visors made:
But oh! what masquers richly dight
Can boast of bosoms half so light!
England was merry England when
Old Christmas brought his sports again.
'Twas Christmas broached the mightiest ale,
'Twas Christmas told the merriest tale;
A Christmas gambol oft would cheer
The poor man's heart through half the year.

Sir Walter Scott.

THE minstrels played their Christmas tune
To-night beneath my cottage-eaves;
While smitten by a lofty moon,
The encircling laurels thick with leaves
Gave back a rich and dazzling sheen,
That overpowered their natural green.

Through hill and valley every breeze
Had sunk to rest with folded wings:
Keen was the air, but could not freeze
Nor check the music of the strings;
So stout and hardy were the band
That scraped the chords with strenuous hand.

And who but listened?—till was paid
Respect to every inmate's claim,

CHRISTMAS MERRYMAKING

The greeting given, the music played
In honour of each household name,
Duly pronounced with lusty call,
And a merry Christmas wished to all.

O Brother, I revere the choice
That took thee from thy native hills;
And it is given thee to rejoice:
Though public care full often tills
(Heaven only witness of the toil)
A barren and ungrateful soil.

Yet would that thou, with me and mine,
Hadst heard this never-failing rite;
And seen on other faces shine
A true revival of the light,
Which Nature, and these rustic powers,
In simple childhood spread through ours!

For pleasure hath not ceased to wait
On these expected annual rounds,
Whether the rich man's sumptuous gate
Call forth the unelaborate sounds,
Or they are offered at the door
That guards the lowliest of the poor.

How touching, when at midnight sweep
Snow-muffled winds and all is dark,
To hear—and sink again to sleep!
Or at an earlier call to mark
By blazing fire, the still suspense
Of self-complacent innocence;

CHRISTMAS MERRYMAKING

The mutual nod, the grave disguise
Of hearts with gladness brimming o'er,
And some unbidden tears that rise
For names once heard, and heard no more;
Tears brightened by the serenade
For infant in the cradle laid!

Ah, not for emerald fields alone
With ambient streams more pure and bright
Than fabled Cytherea's zone
Glittering before the Thunderer's sight,
Is to my heart of hearts endeared
The ground where we were born and reared!

Hail ancient manners! sure defence,
Where they survive, of wholesome laws:
Remnants of love whose modest sense
Thus into narrow room withdraws;
Hail usages of pristine mould,
And ye that guard them, mountains old!

Bear with me, brother! quench the thought
That slights this passion or condemns;
If thee fond fancy ever brought
From the proud margin of the Thames
And Lambeth's venerable towers
To humbler streams and greener bowers.

Yes they can make, who fail to find,
Short leisure even in busiest days;
Moments to cast a look behind,
And profit by those kindly rays

CHRISTMAS MERRYMAKING

That through the clouds do sometimes steal,
And all the far off past reveal.

Hence while the imperial city's din
Beats frequent on thy satiate ear,
A pleased attention I may win
To agitations less severe,
That neither overwhelm nor cloy,
But fill the hollow vale with joy.

William Wordsworth.

WINTER was not unkind because uncouth,
His prisoned time made me a closer guest
And gave thy graciousness a warmer zest,
Biting all else with keen and angry tooth :
And bravelier the triumphant blood of youth
Mantling thy cheek its happy home possest,
And sterner sport by day put strength to test,
And custom's feast at night gave tongue to truth.

Or say hath flaunting summer a device
To match our midnight revelry that rang
With steel and flame along the snow-girt ice?
Or when we harked to nightingales that sang
On dewy eves in spring, did they entice
To gentler love than winter's icy fang?

Robert Bridges.

BALLADE OF CHRISTMAS GHOSTS

BALLADE OF CHRISTMAS GHOSTS

Between the moonlight and the fire
In winter twilights long ago,
What ghosts we raised for your desire,
To make your merry blood run slow!
How old, how grave, how wise we grow!
No Christmas ghost can make us chill,
Save those that troop in mournful row,
The ghosts we all can raise at will!

The beasts can talk in barn and byre
On Christmas Eve, old legends know.
As year by year the years retire,
We men fall silent then I trow,
Such sights hath memory to show,
Such voices from the silence thrill,
Such shapes return with Christmas snow,—
The ghosts we all can raise at will.

Oh, children of the village choir,
Your carols on the midnight throw,
Oh, bright across the mist and mire,
Ye ruddy hearths of Christmas glow!
Beat back the dread, beat down the woe,
Let's cheerily descend the hill;
Be welcome all, to come or go,
The ghosts we all can raise at will!

CHRISTMAS EVE

Envoy.
Friend, sursum corda, soon or slow
We part, like guests who 've joyed their fill ;
Forget them not, nor mourn them so,
The ghosts we all can raise at will.

A. Lang.

CHRISTMAS EVE

Basil. Sandy. Brian. Menzies.

SANDY
In holly hedges starving birds
    Silently mourn the setting year.

BASIL
Upright like silver-plated swords
    The flags stand in the frozen mere.

BRIAN
The mistletoe we still adore
    Upon the twisted hawthorn grows.

MENZIES
In antique gardens hellebore
    Puts forth its blushing Christmas rose.

SANDY
Shrivelled and purple, cheek by jowl,
    The hips and haws hang drearily.

BASIL
Rolled in a ball the sulky owl
    Creeps far into his hollow tree.

CHRISTMAS EVE

BRIAN

In abbeys and cathedrals dim
  The birth of Christ is acted o'er;
The kings of Cologne worship Him,
  Balthazar, Jasper, Melchior.

MENZIES

And while our midnight talk is made
  Of this and that and now and then,
The old earth-stopper with his spade
  And lantern seeks the fox's den.

SANDY

Oh, for a northern blast to blow
  These depths of air that cream and curdle !

BASIL

Now are the halcyon days, you know ;
  Old Time has leapt another hurdle :
And pauses as he only may
  Who knows he never can be caught.

BRIAN

The winter solstice, shortest day
  And longest night, was past, I thought.

BASIL

Oh yes ! but fore-and-aft a week
  Silent the winds must ever be,
Because the happy halcyons seek
  Their nests upon the sea.

162

CHRISTMAS EVE

BRIAN

The Christmas-time! the lovely things
    That last of it! Sweet thoughts and deeds!

SANDY

How strong and green old Legend clings
    Like ivy round the ruined creeds!

MENZIES

A fearless, ruthless, wanton band,
    Deep in our hearts we guard from scathe,
Of last year's log a smouldering brand
    To light at Yule the fire of faith.

BRIAN

The shepherds in the field at night
    Beheld an angel glory-clad,
And shrank away with sore affright.
    'Be not afraid,' the angel bade.

'I bring good news to king and clown,
    To you here crouching on the sward;
For there is born in David's town
    A Saviour which is Christ the Lord.

'Behold the Babe is swathed, and laid
    Within a manger.' Straight there stood
Beside the angel all arrayed
    A heavenly multitude.

'Glory to God,' they sang; 'and peace,
    Good pleasure among men.'

CHRISTMAS EVE

SANDY
The wondrous message of release!

MENZIES
Glory to God again!

BRIAN
Again! God help us to be good!

BASIL
Hush! hark! without; the waits, the waits!
  With brass, and strings, and mellow wood.

MENZIES
A simple tune can ope heaven's gates!

SANDY
Slowly they play, poor careful souls,
  With wistful thoughts of Christmas cheer,
Unwitting how their music rolls
  Away the burden of the year.

BASIL
And with the charm, the homely rune,
  Our thoughts like childhood's thoughts are given,
When all our pulses beat in tune
  With all the stars of heaven.

MENZIES
Oh cease! Oh cease!
164

CHRISTMAS EVE

SANDY

                          Ay; cease, and bring
The wassail-bowl, the cup of grace.

BRIAN
Pour wine, and heat it till it sing,
   With cloves and cardamums and mace.

.   .   .   .

BRIAN
Hush! hark! the waits far up the street!

BASIL
   A distant, ghostly charm unfolds,
Of magic music wild and sweet,
   Anomes and clarigolds.

                          John Davidson.

NOTES

THE six Latin Hymns here given are the best of those upon the Nativity, from the austere simplicity of St. Ambrose, to the rough jolt of the popular carol in the thirteen-syllable trochaic metre. For detailed criticism the reader will consult the authorities on Sacred Latin Poetry; it will suffice here to say that St. Ambrose was bishop of Milan in the fourth century, and though not quite the first writer, was practically the founder, of Latin Hymnology; that Prudentius (born 348) wrote sacred poems from which hymns were extracted for church purposes, and that the Abbé Mauburn was the fifteenth century author of a treatise called 'Rosetum Spirituale,' from which the poem here quoted is taken.

Page 4.—PUER NATUS IN BETHLEHEM is an anonymous poem, the oldest known text of which is found in a Benedictine Processional of the fourteenth century. Verses 6-10 are much later. See Julian, 'Dictionary of Hymnology.'

Page 6.—ADESTE FIDELES, which has been attributed without any authority to St. Bonaventura (born 1221), is of unknown authorship. Mr. Julian considers it as most probably a French or German hymn of the seventeenth or eighteenth century.

Page 9.—ANGELUM MISIT SUUM was printed in Thomas Wright's 'Songs and Carols,' edited for the Percy Society from a MS. in his possession. Mr. Wright was a notoriously careless editor (see an article in the 'Quarterly Review' for 1848 by the father of Dr. Garnett of the British Museum), and the last verse of the carol as printed by him is nonsense. A few obvious blunders in syntax have been corrected throughout the poem, but the following, which is the final stanza, is less corrigible.

O Pater qui genuisti hunc ab initio
Et dedisti gentes sibi pregandes pretio
Hic cum venit quos redemit sanguinis precio
Judicare, fac vitare nos a supplicio.

Dr. Garnett has not been able to ascertain what became of Mr. Wright's MS., so that verification has been impossible.

NOTES

A specimen may be added here of a hybrid style of poem very popular in the fifteenth century.

Ave maris stella,
  The star on the sea,
Dei Mater alma,
  Blessed mot she be,
Atque semper virgo,
  Pray thy son for me,
Felix cœli porta,
  That I may come to thee.
Gabriel, that archangel
  Was the messenger;

So fair he gret our Lady,
  With an 'ave' so clear:
'Hail, be thou, Mary,
  Be thou, Mary,
Full of Goddes grace,
  And Queen of Mercy.'

EARLY CAROLS.—Besides the private MS. edited for the Percy Society, another (in the British Museum, Sloane MS., 2593) was edited by Mr. Wright for the Warton Club. These, both apparently of the reign of Henry VI., are our oldest collections of Christmas Songs and Carols. From the Percy Society reprint I have taken THIS ENDRIS NIGHT, and from the other ST. STEPHEN WAS A CLERK and I SING OF A MAIDEN.

Page 13.—AS JOSEPH WAS A-WALKING, a passage from what is known as 'Cherry Tree Carol.'

Page 14.—NAY, IVY, NAY. First printed in Ritson's 'Ancient Songs and Ballads,' from a MS. of Henry VI.'s reign (Harl. 5396).

Page 16.—IN BETHLEHEM THAT NOBLE PLACE. From 'Christmas Carolles newly imprinted' (c. 1550), as published in 'Bibliographical Miscellanies, being a selection of curious pieces in verse and prose' (1813).

Page 17.—THIS ENDRIS NIGHT. Another poem beginning so is printed in Sandys' 'Christmas Carols.'

Page 25.—William Dunbar, born c. 1460, and the greatest of the old Scottish poets, was originally a preaching friar, and afterwards king's ambassador. His poetry is not always devotional, but it is always well written.

Page 27.—THE BURNING BABE, for which Mr. Crane has drawn one of his happiest illustrations, is the gem of Southwell's poetry; his other Christmas poems being also very favourable specimens. He was a Jesuit priest, and suffered martyrdom with

170

NOTES

great constancy for following his vocation (1595). Among the notes of Ben Jonson's conversations preserved by Drummond of Hawthornden comes the following: 'That Southwell was hanged; yet so he had written that piece of his "The Burning Babe," he would have been content to destroy many of his.'

Page 33.—Jonson's remarks on Donne are also worth quoting. 'He esteemeth John Donne the first poet in the world in some things . . . that Donne for not keeping of accent deserved hanging . . . that Donne himself, for not being understood, would perish.' It is pleasant to see that a modern edition of this fine and forgotten poet is announced for 'The Muses' Library.'

Page 34.—Joseph Hall (born in 1574), was bishop of Exeter and afterwards of Norwich. He was a bold prelate, and incurred the enmity first of Laud, afterwards of the Commonwealth, by whom his see was sequestrated. He spent the last years of his life on a small Norfolk farm. Most of his poetry, written in early life, took the form of satires.

Page 36.—Sir John Beaumont was an elder brother of Francis Beaumont, the dramatist; in politics a Royalist, and in religion a Puritan. His works have been collected by Dr. Grosart in the Fuller Worthies' Library.

Page 39.—William Drummond of Hawthornden, whose conversations with Ben Jonson, who visited him in 1619, have been referred to above, was, in point of art, the Lord de Tabley of the seventeenth century. One of his best pieces, beginning 'Phœbus, arise,' has become familiar to this generation from its inclusion in 'The Golden Treasury.'

Page 41.—George Wither (1588-1667), the author of that fine poem 'The Mistress of Philarete,' in which occurs the popular 'Shall I wasting in despair,' wrote also much religious poetry, very little of which is worth reading. The ROCKING HYMN is from 'Hallelujah' with one verse omitted; the other poem from 'Hymns and Songs of the Church.'

Page 45.—To read Giles Fletcher is to be reminded of both Spenser and Milton, his greater master and his greater disciple. But he has beauties of his own: witness the concluding lines of the excerpt here given from 'Christ's Victory in Heaven.'

Page 46.—The Rev. Robert Herrick was vicar of Dean Prior in Devonshire from 1629 to 1647, when he was ejected by the Puritans,

NOTES

and again from 1662 to his death, twelve years later. His sacred poems or 'Noble Numbers,' as he calls them, have been thrown into the shade by the more secular 'Hesperides,' into which he has transfused the very essence of Devonshire cream; but his religious verse is of genuine if not deep inspiration.

Page 49.—It is matter of regret that Herbert's muse can be represented here by only one piece, and that far from his best.

Page 51.—This marvellous hymn was written by Milton when he was just twenty-one years of age.

Page 61.—The title which the editor gave to Crashaw's poems—'Steps to the Temple'—represents by no means adequately his relation to Herbert. Crashaw's genius was far more fervid, and guided with far less taste. Fervour and bad taste are, indeed, constant notes of Roman Catholic poetry, but Crashaw to these adds genius. The second piece here given is from the 'Sospetto d'Herode.' Of the Epiphany Hymn we have printed only the opening and the close.

Page 71.—Jeremy Taylor told his friend Evelyn that in writing verse he had but the use of his left hand, and the criticism is a just one. He has no mastery of rhythm or even of metre.

Page 73.—Henry Vaughan is another example of a poet marred for want of pains. With a mystical and imaginative mind that could sustain itself in regions to which Herbert could never soar, his attraction to Herbert came too late in life to permit of his mastering that poet's admirable method. The poems on church festivals, to which the scope of this book limits us, are among his poorest.

Page 77.—From 'England's Helicon,' an anthology published in 1600.

Page 79.—Of the anonymous poems, the first two and the last come from the Moravian Hymn-book, and should be traceable to their authors, though I have not succeeded in tracing them. The third was found by Mr. Bullen in a Christ Church MS., and published in 'More Lyrics from Elizabethan Song-books.'

Page 82.—We are sensible of a chill in passing out of the seventeenth century. Tate and Watts, even Doddridge and Wesley, ill make up for the glow and fervour we have left behind.

Page 86.—John Byrom (1692-1763), the writer of at least one fine hymn, and several unequalled epigrams, was a friend of William Law, the mystic, many of whose periods he did into verse. The poem here quoted continues for many lines more, growing prosier as it proceeds.

Page 94.—From 'May Carols,' 1857.

NOTES

Page 100.—Edward Thring (1821-1887) was for thirty-four years headmaster of Uppingham School, which he transformed from an insignificant local grammar-school into a public school of the first rank. His 'Poems and Translations' appeared in 1887.

Page 102.—By special permission of Messrs Macmillan.

Page 103.—MASTERS, IN THIS HALL was first printed in Sedding's 'Antient Christmas Carols (1860).

Page 106.—OUTLANDERS, WHENCE CAME YE LAST? is from 'The Land East of the Sun and West of the Moon,' in vol. iii. of the 'Earthly Paradise.'

Page 108.—SIR GALAHAD is from the 'Defence of Guenevere' volume.

Page 118.—This quaint carol, almost too quaint, as some may think, was suggested by a drawing of D. G. Rossetti's.

Page 121.—This poem is printed for the first time. A few of Father Hopkins's poems were published in Miles' 'Poets of the Century' (vol. viii.), with a brief memoir by Mr. Robert Bridges; a few more will be found in 'Lyra Sacra,' an anthology made by the present editor (Methuens); it is to be hoped that before long his genius may be recognised in a complete edition.

Page 127.—From 'Retrospect.'

Page 131.—From 'A Book of Verses' (George Allen, 1884).

Page 132.—Mr. Image's poem is here first published.

Page 133.—From 'Diversi Colores,' 1891.

Page 135.—From 'The Religion of Humanity and other poems' (Rivington and Percival, 1890).

Page 136.—Two verses from a poem called 'How Love Came,' by Mrs. Alice Archer Sewall, published in 'Harper's Magazine,' Copyright 1893, by Harper and Brothers.

Page 139.—CAPUT APRI DEFERO. This is the oldest and best of the Boar's Head Carols.

Page 141.—Some of the references in Wither's poem are not now to be explained. None of the antiquaries seem to know what the games of Rowland-ho and catching the owls were; noddy is cribbage, and the wildmare probably a see-saw.

Page 148.—TWELFTH NIGHT. A pea and bean were baked in the twelfth cake, and whoever drew them were king and queen respectively.

Page 150.—TO SIR SIMON STEWARD. Tittyries are well ex-

NOTES

plained by Mr. Pollard to be an early club of Mohocks. He cites a poem of a date before 1633, in which the line occurs—'They call themselves the Tytere-tues.' Fox in the hole is a hopping game; Shoeing the mare a kind of fox and hounds. Liber Pater means Father Bacchus.

Page 154.—From 'Marmion.' Introduction to canto vi.

Page 156.—'To the Rev. Dr. Wordsworth, with the sonnets to the River Duddon, and other poems in the collection' (1820).

Page 159.—From the 'Growth of Love' (privately printed by Rev. H. Daniel, Oxford, 1889).

Page 160.—From 'Rhymes à la Mode' (Paul and Trench, 1885).

Page 161.—From 'Fleet Street Eclogues' (Mathews and Lane, 1893), with an omission sanctioned by Mr. Davidson.